LIBRARY

ACTING & THEATRE

Cheryl Evans and Lucy Smith
Edited by Cheryl Evans

Designed by Jane Felstead

Drama consultants: Dr. Nick Kaye, Joint School of Theatre Studies, University of Warwick and Mike Morrison, Head of English, Monmouth School, Monmouth, Gwent.

Acting photographs by Helen Putsman; make-up by Karen Purvis
Illustrated by Conny Jude, Guy Smith, Bob Moulder, Barry Jones, Ian Bott
Hand-lettering by Solos Solou

Contents

With special thanks to the actors: Lara Bobroff, Alyson Coleman, Marva Donaldson, Miles Guerrini, Robin Hellier, Kamini Khanduri, Mark Leadbetter, Jeremy Nicholls, Melissa Palmer, Anita Qadri, Emma Randall, Emma Reeves and Jacob Yapp.

Dance wear for photographs by Gamba, 3, Garrick St., London WC2.
Thanks also to The City of London School and The Central School of Speech and Drama for help with this project.

Universal Edition

Acting and the theatre

Throughout history, in every country and culture, people have enjoyed putting on and watching performances. Plays do more than just tell a story, they bring it to life vividly. As they entertain, they also tell you about new ideas, other people and yourself.

In this book, you can read about all the people and skills involved in a theatre production, from actors to lighting and sound technicians, set designers and builders, costume and make-up people and how the director co-ordinates them all.

Theatre also means buildings, which have taken many forms over the centuries. The history of theatre on pages 44-48 explains about this, and you can find out how a modern theatre is run on pages 52-53. The Oriental theatre section (pages 49-51) shows how much traditions vary in different parts of the world.

This book also tells you about the people, plays and ideas that have influenced drama as it is today, and about how you can get involved.

Acting and drama

Acting in a show is a terrific thrill and everyone involved in a performance learns about responsibility, teamwork and the excitement of creating something.

Dressing up is part of the fun of acting.

Acting is used in other ways, too. In schools and other groups, people explore problems and situations that concern them by acting them out. Afterwards they discuss their meaning and importance and how they feel about them.

A mock job interview can boost your confidence and make the real thing less scary.

Amateur and professional

If you are a professional, you earn your living in the theatre. There is more about the jobs you can do and how to qualify on pages 56-57.

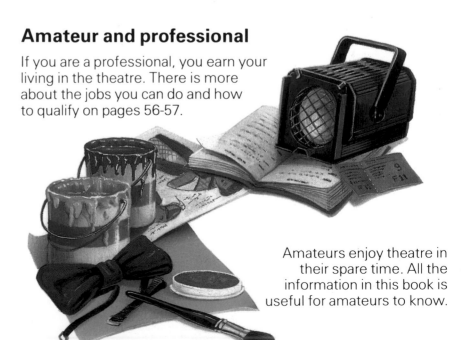

Amateurs enjoy theatre in their spare time. All the information in this book is useful for amateurs to know.

Fit to act

The first part of this book is about how actors train.

An actor needs to be as fit and supple as possible. All acting is physically demanding and it may involve dancing, fighting or other energetic activities, too.

Acting can also be emotionally draining, which causes tension. A tense body is more likely to make awkward movements and perhaps get hurt.

Actors need special training for stage fights like this. They usually get coaching from professionals.

Warming up

Before rehearsing or performing, actors always do warm-up exercises. This means gently stretching and relaxing to get rid of tension and loosen up. The routine on this page makes a good overall warm-up. If you want to try any of the acting exercises in this book, you should warm up like this first.

◀ 1. Stand with your feet about 45cm (18in) apart. Raise yourself up on your toes. Now drop down onto your heels. Repeat.

◀ 2. Draw your shoulders up to your ears, then let them drop.

◀ 3. Gently drop your head forwards, then slowly roll it one way, then the other.

▼ 4. Lean sideways. Slide your hand down your leg. Bounce gently from the waist to go down further.

5. Rotate each shoulder in turn in a big circle.

▲
6. Breathe in, stand on tiptoe and stretch your arms up. Breathe out and flop down.

7. Pull each ▶ knee in towards your waist.

Do it both sides. ◀

Try not to lean forwards or back.

Let your head flop over, too.

◀ 8. Circle your wrists, then each ankle, around both ways and finally shake out all your limbs as if trying to fling them away.

Movement

There are no set rules for how to act. But there are exercises and activities that help actors develop the skills they need.

An actor's voice and body are his two main tools. He needs to learn about moving and speaking to communicate well with an audience.

His relaxed stance and vacant stare are nonchalant, or perhaps he is avoiding confrontation.

Her dreamy look and thoughtful stirring seem sad or preoccupied.

He is jumping up snarling and pointing aggressively.

Learning to look

In order to play people other than themselves convincingly, actors must watch how people behave: how they sit, stand, gesture and move. This kind of body language says a lot about what someone is like and how they feel.

You can become aware of body language by watching people in everyday places. In this picture you can "read" some tell-tale signs. Practise interpreting people's mood or personality from their body language when you go out.

The space between

Acting usually involves interaction between characters. One thing that tells you a lot about how they feel about each other and affects how they relate is the distance between them. This exercise shows how this can work. Do it and see if you feel the effect.

1. In a large room, or outside, two of you stand well apart.

2. One of you stands still, while the other walks slowly up to you. Try to notice how you feel as you get closer.

3. Do it again. This time the still person says "stop" each time she senses a change in your relationship.

At the start you just have a general view of each other.

Now you start to distinguish his face clearly.

Here you make eye contact for the first time. You might feel the need to acknowledge each other.

Stop

Stop

Stop

Stop

Stop

This would be a good distance for a friendly conversation.

This feels too close unless you are being really aggressive or affectionate.

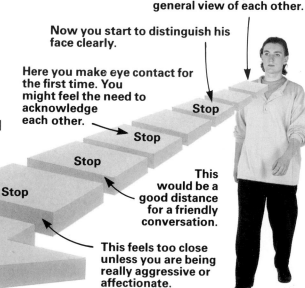

Laban's theory

To help them think clearly about different movements and how they affect the impression you make and the way you behave, actors often study the work of Hungarian choreographer Rudolph von Laban. He defined eight basic kinds of movement. Here they are, with things you can do to feel how they differ.

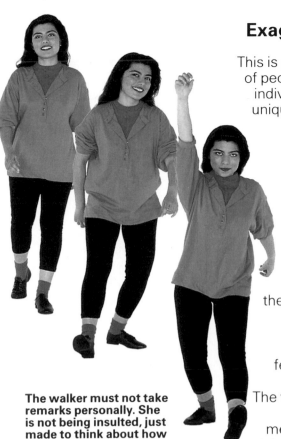

Exaggerated walk

This is an exercise a group of people can do to make individuals aware of the uniqueness of their way of walking.

Everyone stands in a circle, then one person walks around the inside of the circle in front of them.

People watch and call out things they notice about how she walks: if she swings her arms oddly, or sticks her feet up, for instance.

The walker exaggerates the things they mention. Each person takes a turn at walking.

The walker must not take remarks personally. She is not being insulted, just made to think about how she walks.

Copy-cat walk

To go a stage further, the actors, in pairs, walk closely one behind the other. The rear one tries to copy exactly the front one's walk. Try this yourself with a friend. See if it makes you feel different to walk like someone else.

Punch. Make a fist and punch the air hard.

Press. Put your palms on a wall and push.

Dab. Knock lightly once on a door.

Glide. Smooth crumpled paper or cloth.

Flick. Lightly click your fingers.

Float. Walk lightly on your toes.

Slash. Whip the air with your arm.

Wring. Wring a towel really hard.

Laban called these eight kinds of movements "efforts" and described them using words from the pairs of opposites shown below. He called these "qualities".

Laban's qualities.

Direct: Indirect

Light: Heavy

Sustained: Unsustained

The qualities of a punch, say, are *Direct* (in one direction), *Heavy* (a strong movement) and *Unsustained* (one action that then stops).

A float's qualities are *Indirect* (wandering), *Light* (airy) and *Sustained* (continuing).

Do the efforts again and see if you can feel these qualities.

Movement and sound

The way you move affects the way you speak. Some of the efforts, such as the wring, slash, glide or punch involve your whole body. Yawn to relax your voice, then try the efforts while making a long yawning sound. Try changing from one effort to another. See how the sound changes.

5

Voice

Just as actors learn about their body and how it moves, they also learn about their voice, how it works and ways to control it. Actors use their voice all the time and may also have to sing, or seem to shout or whisper, and still be heard clearly. To do this without strain, their voice must be well-trained. These are the kinds of exercises they use. You can try most of them.

Being relaxed

Actors always warm up before voice work. A tense body makes a tense voice, which is less flexible and more likely to get tired. Ideally, they do a general warm-up first (see page 3), then extra relaxation, as shown below.

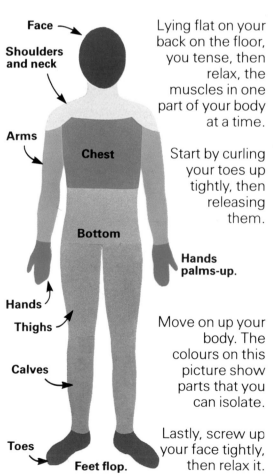

Face

Shoulders and neck

Arms

Chest

Bottom

Hands

Thighs

Calves

Toes

Feet flop.

Hands palms-up.

Lying flat on your back on the floor, you tense, then relax, the muscles in one part of your body at a time.

Start by curling your toes up tightly, then releasing them.

Move on up your body. The colours on this picture show parts that you can isolate.

Lastly, screw up your face tightly, then relax it.

Breathing deeply

Your voice is made by your breath vibrating your vocal cords. The more breath you have and the better you control it, the more you can do with your voice. Here's how to practise getting more breath.

If you feel dizzy, wait before trying again.

Your vocal cords are in your voice box, in your throat.

Lungs

Diaphragm

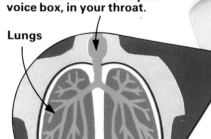

This hand is on a muscle called the diaphragm, which stretches across under your ribs.

Lie flat on your back on the floor. Put one hand on your chest and breathe slowly and deeply in and out. Feel your hand rise and fall.

Now put the other hand just below your rib-cage. Breathe in again. This time, once your chest has risen, try to make your other hand rise.

Saving your breath

Forming the habit of breathing deeply takes practice. Here's a way of learning to control a deep breath as it is released.

Lying down, draw a slow, deep breath. Breathe out saying "Aaaah" for as long as you can.

Notice how the strength and quality of the sound change as you run out of breath.

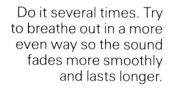

Do it several times. Try to breathe out in a more even way so the sound fades more smoothly and lasts longer.

Flickering flame

This is another exercise for breath control.

Take a deep breath, then breathe out across a candle flame without blowing it out.

You have to release your breath very gently and evenly.

Projecting your voice

Projecting your voice means being heard clearly without shouting. It has as much to do with good articulation (saying words clearly) and correct emphasis (stressing words so that their meaning is clear), as volume. Training your voice can improve projection.

A sound play

Here's a way to explore the effect sounds have in a space. A few people sit in the centre of a space and close their eyes. Others plan a scene and try to evoke it using only voices (but not words) and other noises they make themselves. Here's how it might go.

Making sounds

Your lips and tongue shape your voice as it comes out of your mouth. This exercise makes you think about sounds and how you make them. It helps you to speak clearly and not trip over words that are hard to say.

Yawn, making a yawning noise as you do it. Make the noise continue until you have breathed out completely.

Do it again. This time change the noise by making shapes with your mouth, as shown in these pictures.

Now try saying these sequences. Fill your lungs first:

beh, teh, deh
neh, leh, deh
neh, peh, deh
beh, meh

These are vowel sounds.

Can you feel the difference between these sounds? Think where your tongue and lips go to make each one.

The first actor establishes that he is asleep.

Another actor makes a loud alarm clock noise close to the audience to startle them.

Z-Z-Z-Z

YAWN

The first actor yawns to show he is waking up.

He walks, slapping on his bare feet, around the audience.

Audience

The audience can be just one person.

BEEP! BEEP!

Afterwards, they discuss what they thought was happening and how effective the sounds were.

In a new place, the first actor starts a shushing sound for shower water.

From a distance, a third actor makes a doorbell ringing noise.

BRRRRING

SHHHHHH

Huh? Grrrr...

The first actor stops the shower noise as if he's turned it off, and mutters in annoyance.

The story would continue from here.

Loud and soft noises, from near or far away, human and non-human, paint a vivid picture of the story and the space where it is happening.

7

Theatre games

When people first start to act, or some actors get together for the first time, they may feel a bit inhibited. Good drama teachers and directors know this and take time to help a group get to know and trust each other. A good way to do this is with theatre games, such as those shown here.

Fruit salad

1. Everyone sits in a circle on the floor. One person in the middle is the caller. They all, including the caller, take the names of kinds of fruit.

2. The caller shouts the names of two or more of the fruit. The people who 'are' these fruit jump up and swap places.

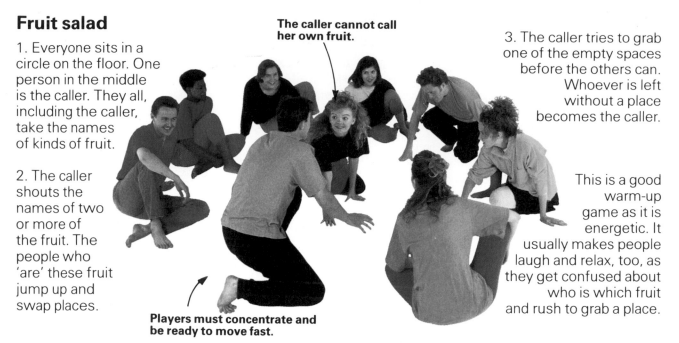

The caller cannot call her own fruit.

Players must concentrate and be ready to move fast.

3. The caller tries to grab one of the empty spaces before the others can. Whoever is left without a place becomes the caller.

This is a good warm-up game as it is energetic. It usually makes people laugh and relax, too, as they get confused about who is which fruit and rush to grab a place.

Pulsing

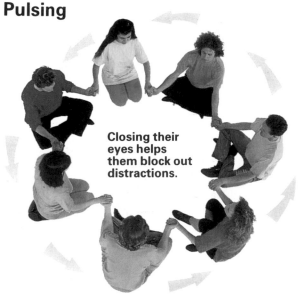

Closing their eyes helps them block out distractions.

All sit in a circle, joining hands. One person starts by squeezing the hand of his neighbour on the right. The neighbour immediately does the same, and so on around the circle. Once the game gets going, the squeezes feel like a pulse of energy uniting the group.

Trust

Actors' physical safety and willingness to express powerful or painful emotions depend on being able to trust the people they work with. This exercise helps develop trust.

Two people of roughly equal size and weight stand one behind the other, about a pace apart.

The one in front leans back on her heels, keeping her body straight but not rigid.

This person must not be afraid of falling.

It becomes a relaxing, rocking sensation.

She must be sure to catch securely and push gently each time.

The one behind supports her partner's back with the palms of her hands as she leans backwards, then pushes her gently upright again. The one in front rocks back and forwards several times.

Blind faith

This is another trust game. One person is blindfolded. The other guides her around from behind, by just a light touch on her shoulders. They must not speak.

They may set up an obstacle course of rubbish bins, chairs and so on.

It is disconcerting to be suddenly blind. This game teaches you to entrust your safety to someone else.

At first she is nervous and uncertain.

Gradually, she gains confidence and can walk more quickly.

The mirror game

Two people stand quite close, facing each other. One of them begins to make slow movements, such as raising an arm. The other tries to mirror exactly each move the first person makes.

This person lifts her right arm to mirror her partner's left arm.

At first he just moves one part of his body at a time but later he makes more complex movements.

Then they swap roles and the other person leads. In the end, they should be so in tune that they make and reflect each other's moves without knowing who is leading. This teaches mutual give and take.

Gobbledegook

This is a game that warms up your voice as well as making you respond to each other.

Two people start a conversation in nonsense words.

They see if they can get a sense of what the "conversation" is about and develop it.

Naa, gloop-gloop.. bah....dibble.... pup....

Yo hu! pa dink spling yabba flip....

He looks and sounds depressed. He shakes his head and makes gloomy noises.

His partner is perkier, as if trying to cheer him up.

Gestures and expressions say as much as "words".

Learning to improvise

Improvisation, or impro, means making up actions and words as you go along. Improvising helps actors to imagine being different people in all sorts of circumstances. They can try out acting styles and develop their skills.

First impros

Improvising seems hard at first, but you can start with simple impros like these. In the first impro there are no words, so actors can concentrate on their actions. The second uses cards to help get started. Usually, a group leader guides impros, but both of these are easy enough for a few people to try on their own.

Production line

Actions must be strong and repeatable.

The line should develop a rhythm that's a bit like a factory at work.

One person starts doing a simple, mechanical action and making a suitable noise to go with it.

The next person joins in with a new action and noise. She tries to link it in with the first person's.

Others join the line one at a time. This impro gets a group used to responding to each other and co-operating.

Character cards

Improvisation allows actors to portray a variety of characters and emotions without working on an actual play text. They cannot start from nothing, though, so an impro like this gives them a starting point.

In a large group, it can be done by a few people at a time, while the rest watch.

The leader writes character traits, such as shy, bossy or impatient, on cards.

Actors pick a card at random. The leader suggests a scene, such as waiting for a bus that is late.

The actors try to behave as a character with the trait they have picked might in this situation.

10

Developing impro skills

The main qualities needed for good impros are quick reactions, co-operation with others and being able to accept what other people do and build on it to keep the impro flowing. Here are some impros that develop these skills.

Freeze

One person starts to mime a simple activity. The rest of the group try to guess what he is doing.

This actor mimes painting a wall. He bends to refill his brush, then stretches up to paint.

Once they have guessed, the group leader shouts "Freeze" and the actor freezes.

The leader tries to pick a time when the actor's pose is interesting.

Another actor comes and takes up the frozen pose. This actor now starts a new mime inspired by the pose.

The second actor mimes conducting an orchestra. The first actor rejoins the group.

A third actor takes over and begins to waltz with an imaginary partner.

The impro carries on. A new actor takes over each time the leader shouts "Freeze".

This impro develops quick-thinking and ingenuity. Actors must accept what has gone before and think of something new on the spot.

Setting a scene

In this impro, a group works together to evoke the sights and sounds of a place as faithfully as possible. It is vital that no-one tries to dominate or do inappropriate things just to grab attention. These actors are improvising a beach scene.

Some actors may naturally become the focus of attention. These two pointing out to sea and discussing what they see, for example, might attract interest.

This person crosses the scene as a passer-by.

Actors not drawn into the action still contribute as much to the scene and should act just as thoroughly.

He is rolling his trousers up to paddle.

These two are intent on building sandcastles.

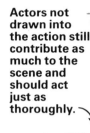

11

More about impro

Impro can be used in many different ways as actors become more confident. A good session usually begins with actors discussing why they are doing the impro, and ends by talking about what they learned from it. Impro is most vivid when people do not plan ahead, but really listen to other actors and respond spontaneously to what has happened just before.

More ways to improvise

Impro is not always group work. Actors may improvise alone, though they usually need someone to watch and guide them. Here are two examples.

Solo speech

The actor says out loud all the thoughts going through his character's head, when he is making a decision, for instance.

> If I go she'll be upset.

> But I really can't stay.

> I could make an excuse....

Solo mime

Even when an actor is alone on stage, he is acting. The personality of his character and the mood he is in should come across in his body language.

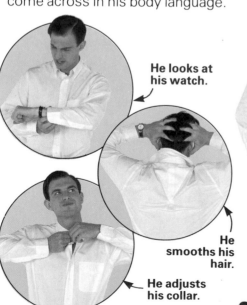

He looks at his watch.

He smooths his hair.

He adjusts his collar.

He taps his toe in frustration.

Mother and father discussing their feelings.

Son moaning to daughter about their parents.

Son and friends comparing their parents.

Improvising a play

Impro can be used to write plays. A group of people decide on a subject, then think of scenes to improvise that show different views of it, or raise interesting questions about it.

For example, to improvise a play about the problems between parents and children, here are some scenes you could act out.

If you record the impros, you can write down the best bits later and discuss ways to link them into a good play.

The things this actor does tell you that he is waiting impatiently for someone and that he is a bit nervous about what he looks like. Actors can practise impros like these in class. They are also useful in rehearsals. An actor can work out the motives of his character in a difficult scene, or try out moves that communicate how he feels to an audience without speaking.

Playing status

An impro such as the Character cards on page 10 is a good way to start, but only creates simplified characters because just one aspect of their personality is given. The exercises below show how impro can become highly sophisticated and be used to develop complex characters that can interact with each other in the subtle way that people do in real life.

Status numbers

In this impro, a number expresses a character's strength of personality, importance and ability to influence others.

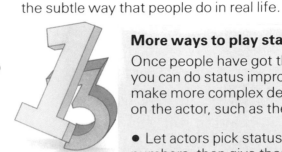

A status number of one indicates an extremely weak, submissive type.

A status number of ten means a very dominant, powerful, persuasive person.

All the numbers between denote subtle gradations between the most dominant and the weakest.

Status impro

Numbers 1 to 10 are written on separate cards, which are then shuffled, face down.

Actors pick a card at random, look at the number, and remember it.

They begin to walk around and, as they meet, they behave as someone with their status number would. It's best done first without words.

Someone watching can try to line the actors up in order of status. It's hardest to sort out close numbers, such as 5 and 7.

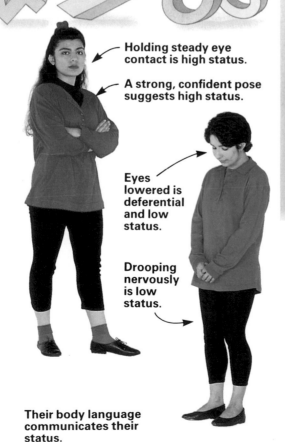

Holding steady eye contact is high status.

A strong, confident pose suggests high status.

Eyes lowered is deferential and low status.

Drooping nervously is low status.

Their body language communicates their status.

More ways to play status

Once people have got the idea, you can do status impros that make more complex demands on the actor, such as these.

● Let actors pick status numbers, then give them a specific role. They must express their status in a way that suits the role: how would the behaviour of a teacher with high status differ from that of a footballer with the same status, for example?

● Try a scene in which a character's status number conflicts with his social status: how might a high status chauffeur talk to a wealthy businessman with low status, for instance?

● Change a character's status in the middle of an impro. See how this affects the outcome.

● Take a simple piece of text and play it with different status combinations. Which are most effective?

Changing status

A person's status changes depending on who he is with. The same person could have high status at home, low status at work and medium status in a sport's team, say.

Status in plays

Working out the relative status of characters in a play can tell you how speech or action should be interpreted.

Building a character

The impro work on the previous pages is good groundwork for learning to play roles. Here you can see ways to develop this into acting fully rounded characters that an audience will find believable and interesting. Actors often find it easier to practise these techniques in class before applying them to a part in a play.

Hot-seating

This is a way for an actor to invent a character that she can then explore and develop, with the help of a group.

The person who is going to create a character sits surrounded by other members of the group. She is in the "hot-seat".

One at a time, people ask her questions. From her answers, a character gradually emerges. The questions delve deeper as the character takes shape.

The actor in the hot-seat starts with no preconceived ideas. The character only develops from the questions and answers. In this way, the whole group helps build the character.

Could you steal a large sum of money?

Questions like these are harder to answer but reveal more.

The person in the hot-seat answers as the character, saying "I" in her replies.

Did you get on well with your mother?

These simple questions establish straightforward facts.

What's your name?

How old are you?

Hot-seat ideas

If the actor finds it hard to start from nothing, she may take a name and basic details from a newspaper story, for instance, and start to build her character from there.

Hot-seating is a good way to invent characters for an improvised play (see page 12).

Other ways to look at characters

The methods described above help an actor explore a character and feel what it is like to be that person. The actor may become deeply involved with the role.

In recent years, some actors and directors have felt that it is more effective to be more detached when acting. They have found various ways to achieve this.

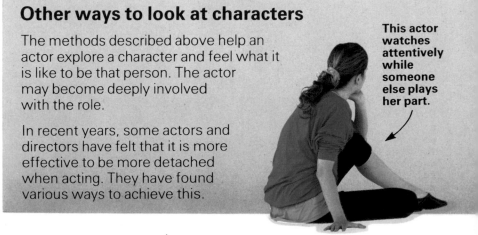

This actor watches attentively while someone else plays her part.

Dressing the part

The actor can take her hot-seated character further by thinking about what she would wear in given circumstances.

Would she be more at home in a slinky evening dress or practical, hard-wearing clothes?

Does she choose bright colours or muted tones?

Would she be more likely to wear stiletto heels, sensible shoes or Wellingtons?

She could try on different things to see which make her look, feel and move most like the character. Once she has decided, these things become part of the character and help her to step into it whenever she puts them on.

The perfect prop

She can do the same thing with props, taking time to consider what would really add to her characterisation. The hot-seat technique can be used again to question the character about the prop and what it means to her.

It is important to find exactly the right thing. A rich old man might use a beautiful, gold-topped, fountain pen, while an impoverished artist writes with a pencil stub, for example.

One example is for actors to swap roles and watch someone else play their part. They can stand back and judge the character as an audience would.

Playing another part helps this actor view the scene from another angle, too.

The German playwright and director, Bertolt Brecht, worked on this approach to acting and wrote a lot about his theories. Read more about this on pages 42-43.

Using impro

Once an actor has established a character that she feels she knows really well, she can take part in impros as that character.

In rehearsal

When you have a part in a play, you need to search for every character clue you can find. Look at what the cast list and stage directions say, what other characters say about yours, and what the things your character says and does reveal.

You can also hot-seat with the part you are playing in mind. This is most useful at later rehearsals when you already know your character well, but want to add depth to your portrayal.

Why were you so angry when I said that?

The questions are specific to the action of the play. →

Do you think you are jealous of your brother?

It can help to improvise a scene that is mentioned in the play but is not shown on stage, such as an earlier meeting between characters or an incident from their past.

You might impro the scene. ↘

I remember you whispering and giggling that night.

Learning lines

Learning lines is crucial to being in a play, yet it can seem like hard work. Here are some hints on how to do it, although there is much more to approaching the words of a play than learning them parrot-fashion.

Looking at language

It is most important to understand all the words. Check unfamiliar ones in a dictionary.

If there is more than one meaning, discuss which is the right one in context.

Plays written in the past may have words that are no longer used or whose sense has changed. These deserve special attention.

Historic texts often have footnotes to explain what words and references meant when they were written.

Some plays are in verse, which is like poetry, though it does not always rhyme. It is often rich in images that can be interpreted in many ways.

Shakespeare and Molière both wrote in verse, for example. Modern playwrights, such as T.S. Eliot did, too.

Most modern plays are written in apparently simple, everyday language, but this often has hidden meanings. To find these, you have to examine who says them, and why.

Won't someone take notice of me?

I'd love a cup of tea.

What he says is direct, but what he means is not.

Word patterns

The meaning of individual words is not the only clue to the real sense of a speech. The way words are grouped by punctuation reveals a lot about how they are meant to be said.

> She should have died hereafter.
> There would have been a time for such a word –
> Tomorrow, and tomorrow, and tomorrow
> Creeps in this petty pace from day to day
> To the last syllable of recorded time;

This is part of a speech by Macbeth, in Shakespeare's play, *Macbeth* (Act V, Scene 5), just after his wife has died. To see how it should be said, say it aloud, including the punctuation, like this:

> She should have died hereafter full stop
> There would have been a time for such a word dash
> Tomorrow comma and tomorrow comma and tomorrow . . .and so on.

Say it again. This time leave a silence for each punctuation mark. Count one silently for a comma, for example, and two for full stops.

> She should have died hereafter one, two
> There would have been a time for such a word one
> Tomorrow one and tomorrow one and tomorrow . . .and so on.

.	**Full stop**	,	**Comma**
:	**Colon**	;	**Semi-colon**
?	**Question mark**	–	**Dash**
!	**Exclamation mark**		

These deserve a count of two.

These only need a count of one.

These exercises also make you aware of how sound and silence work together in speech. Notice, too, the effect of short, abrupt phrases or long, flowing ones and the impression made by repeated words or sounds.

Sound patterns

To examine the sound of words further, try this:

Whisper a speech to yourself. Concentrate on the sounds you hear most clearly and the impression they make.
Try it with Macbeth's speech. Here's how it continues.

And all our yesterdays have lighted fools
The way to dusty death. Out, out, brief candle!
Life's but a walking shadow, a poor player
That struts and frets his hour upon the stage
And then is heard no more. It is a tale
Told by an idiot, full of sound and fury,
Signifying nothing.

Whispering emphasizes hard consonants like p, d and k. A lot of these together make the words sound harsh.

Hissing noises like s, sh and ch are softer and suggest whispers, even at normal volume.

Stage directions

These are words that are in the text, but are not intended to be said. They may describe the set or say what a character is doing or how he should say the words.

ANNA (*angrily*): How can you?

The actor could say this in many ways. The stage direction tells her what the author intended.

SWIFT: Well, what do you think? (*He pours himself a drink*)

To interpret this stage direction the actor must know more about Swift from the play. He must decide whether Swift pours a drink because he is thirsty, because he wants to turn his back or because he is an alcoholic, for example.

Stage directions are as much part of the play as the speeches. They give clues as to how the author sees the set and the characters.

How to learn lines

The cast must know their lines before they can act freely, move about and make eye contact. So lines should be learned as soon as possible.

However, it is best not to learn them before rehearsing a little and getting to know the plot and characters. Otherwise, you risk learning them mechanically, which will be obvious to an audience. You learn lines more easily when you understand them, in any case.

Here are a few tips that some actors find useful:

● Record your lines on a cassette and play them when cooking, jogging, taking a bath and so on.

● Try to visualize the lines on the page.

● Link lines to what you do on stage and think through actions and words together.

● Repeat them last thing before you go to sleep.

If the text is your own, you can underline your part.

Learn to recognize your cues (the last words before you speak).

Clarifying the meaning

Words in a play must be looked at in context. This means who says them, to whom, why, what leads up to them and what is said or done next. Each speech must be said in a way that is consistent with other things a character says and does.

The importance of emphasis and intonation to understanding has already been mentioned in Projecting your voice (page 7). Here are some clues on finding the right words to stress, called key words. Look for:
● Words that are repeated.
● Words that build up a special effect or image through their sounds or meanings.
● Words at the start or end of a sentence.

Mime

When most people think of mime they think of a white-faced, silent clown, like the most famous modern example, Marcel Marceau. In fact, this is just one style of mime. Mime is always a physical, even acrobatic performance, but need not necessarily be done without words.

Studying mime

It is not just people who want to be mime artistes who study mime. Mime concentrates on the body and movement and is useful to all actors. These exercises give a first taste of mime skills. As mime is so physical, warm up well before trying them.

Slo-mo run

Here's a way to start analysing more closely your everyday actions. ▶

Does your head move?

How do your legs and arms move?

In a large room, or outside, run around as fast as you can. Then try to run in slow motion over a metre (3ft) or less. Move your weight forward slowly and continuously. Try to recall exactly what running felt like.

When are your knees bent or straight?

"In the manner of"

Do the washing.

He tries to wash up "angrily".

Angrily

Someone calls out this action.

This game makes you think about how movement communicates your feelings.

One person thinks of an adverb, such as quietly, angrily, boldly and so on.

The others call out actions for him to mime "in the manner of" his adverb.

He must do the activities in such a way that the others can guess the adverb.

This exercise expands on the ideas in Body language on page 4 and Solo mime on page 12. Even odd combinations, such as "writing a letter greedily" should be tried.

Qualities

You can go further by trying to use only one part of your body to express qualities people can have.

Write some qualities on scraps of paper.

Friendly cheeky Nosy

Qualities.

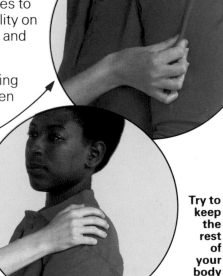

Each person takes a paper, then tries to mime the quality on it using hands and arms only.

Try it again using head, legs, then your whole body.

Spiteful hands might pinch someone.

Kindly hands might pat someone gently.

Try to keep the rest of your body still.

18

Mime and masks

Many kinds of mask are used in mime and other performances. Whether you speak or not when wearing it, your body must move in a way that suits the mask.

Neutral masks are plain and have no expression or character.

Character masks have their own qualities which the actor must bring to life.

Commedia dell'Arte is a traditional type of mime that uses masks (see page 46).

A clown's painted face and red nose are a kind of mask.

Making a mask

If your face is covered and you don't talk, you can only "speak" with your body. That's why wearing masks involves mime skills.

You can make a mask using paper, scissors, sticky tape and ribbon.

Paint the mask, make holes for the eyes and stick ribbon to the sides to tie it on.

Working with a mask

Once you have a mask, you must get to know it. Study it. Does it evoke a character or qualities?

Now put it on and look in a mirror. How does it make you feel?

Try out ways of standing, walking and moving that the mask suggests to you. Which suit the mask best?

Try some of Laban's efforts (page 5) to see which seem appropriate.

You need a full-length mirror for mime work.

You may have to try lots of things before finding something that feels right.

Group work with masks

In a group, individuals get to know their own mask first. Then they can start interacting, like this.

Actors lie on the floor. Their mask characters are "asleep". Then they "wake up" and begin to meet and greet each other for the first time. They react to each other in the character of their mask.

They may try to work out an order of status for the masks (see page 12).

The mask characters wake up in different ways.

They begin to look around and react to what they see.

Only the eye shapes on these masks give the actors clues to develop characters from.

The set

When it is not in use, a stage is just an empty space. When a play is on, a special acting area is usually created on the stage. This defined and decorated area is known as the set. It may represent a particular place, or just provide different levels and spaces for actors to work on and in. Here you can see some of the things that can be used to make a set.

This is the back view of a typical set made with flats (see below.)

The frame is made very firm, as scenery must not wobble.

Every part of the set must be fireproofed.

The side seen by the audience is painted.

This shows how a brace hooks to the frame.

There are special flats with window and door spaces.

This rope, called a throw-line, is wound around hooks called cleats to tie two flats together.

Wooden braces, hooked into the frame and supported by heavy weights, hold the flats up.

Building the set

Skilled theatre carpenters work from the set designer's models and sketches (see pages 22-23) to create the set. One of the basic elements they can use are flats. These are oblong wooden frames with canvas stretched over them and nailed on. The canvas is then painted and the flats are joined together and supported, as shown above, to make "walls" that define the shape of the set. You can see more ways to use flats below.

Box set

This is a box set. Flats make three sides of a room. The audience looks in from the fourth side.

Screen

Flats joined together and covered on both sides form a screen that stands up on its own. With different scenes on each side, you can turn it around for a quick scene change. This is a cheap and versatile way to make a set.

Groundrows

Flats laid on their sides make low scenery called groundrows. Plywood shapes can be nailed to them.

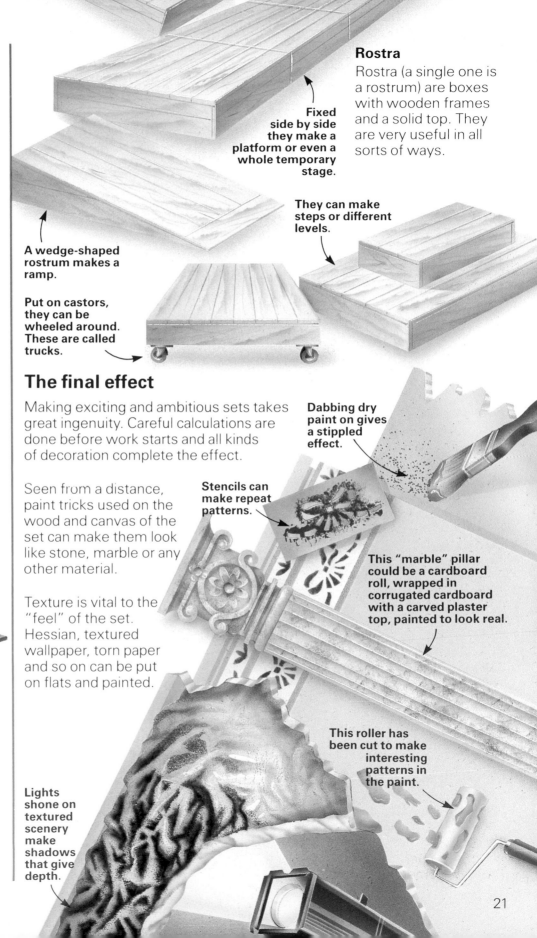

Backdrops

Backdrops are painted cloths hung across the stage as scenery. They can be raised and lowered by ropes and pulleys from bars in the space above the stage.

This space is called the flies.

This backdrop is being flown.

Cyclorama

This is the backdrop the audience would see at the moment.

Stage

A cyclorama is a special backdrop at the back of the stage. It is a screen of stretched white material. Slides and light effects, such as clouds, can be projected onto it.

Rostra

Rostra (a single one is a rostrum) are boxes with wooden frames and a solid top. They are very useful in all sorts of ways.

Fixed side by side they make a platform or even a whole temporary stage.

They can make steps or different levels.

A wedge-shaped rostrum makes a ramp.

Put on castors, they can be wheeled around. These are called trucks.

The final effect

Making exciting and ambitious sets takes great ingenuity. Careful calculations are done before work starts and all kinds of decoration complete the effect.

Seen from a distance, paint tricks used on the wood and canvas of the set can make them look like stone, marble or any other material.

Texture is vital to the "feel" of the set. Hessian, textured wallpaper, torn paper and so on can be put on flats and painted.

Dabbing dry paint on gives a stippled effect.

Stencils can make repeat patterns.

This "marble" pillar could be a cardboard roll, wrapped in corrugated cardboard with a carved plaster top, painted to look real.

This roller has been cut to make interesting patterns in the paint.

Lights shone on textured scenery make shadows that give depth.

Set design

The set is usually the first thing people see at the start of a play, so it sets the tone for the whole performance and should be designed to make a powerful impact. A set designer's job is to devise an imaginative set that is also practical. She must keep to a budget and work within the limits of the available space.

Clues to the set

A play's author nearly always gives some clues about what the set should be like. He may describe a room in detail, or give a general idea, such as "in a sunny square". There may be elements needed to make the plot work, such as more than one door so characters can come and go without meeting, for example.

Neutral set

This set has different levels and areas to act in, but no actual scenery.

Actors bring on and take off individual props as needed.

Actors, costumes and lights will make colours and shapes on this neutral background.

Set styles

Within the needs of the plot, the director knows what style of set he wants. A symbolic set, for example, uses colours and shapes to enhance the play's meaning. A naturalistic set is as life-like as possible. An unadorned set like the one above is called neutral.

Working in the space

The set design must suit the space in which it is to work. The size of stage, storage space and what technical equipment is available are all important. If the set is to tour, it must be easy to set up and strike (take down), and adaptable to different venues.

Sightlines

Any set design has to take into account that the whole audience must be able to see. The views people get of the stage from every corner of the theatre are called sightlines, and the set must not obscure them. On a traditional stage, sightlines and any set design problems they pose are well-known. In other spaces, they must be worked out each time.

Set design problems

A traditional stage is quite easy to design for, as its potential and limitations soon become known to designers. Being original is often the main problem. It is also hard to draw the audience into the set as the rows of seating encourage watching rather than involvement.

The set makes a picture, framed by an arch called the proscenium.

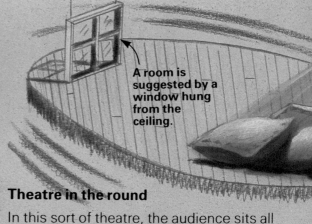

A room is suggested by a window hung from the ceiling.

Theatre in the round

In this sort of theatre, the audience sits all around a central acting space. Normal scenery would block sightlines, so scenes have to be suggested by just a few props and furniture or by lighting different areas or changing colours.

The design

As well as all the information mentioned already, the designer must know about set-building and materials so she can be sure her design is possible to realize.

To get ideas for sets, she must get to know the play thoroughly and research its author and the era in which it takes place. Set locations, the personalities of the play's central characters and the general mood of the piece may suggest ideas for dominant colours or themes.

Material collected from museums, libraries, historic buildings and so on that is relevant to the play's setting can provide inspiration.

There may be several models if there are lots of scene changes.

Cut-out figures in scale show the proportions of the set.

A floor plan of the set can be useful as well.

Costumes must be designed to fit in with the colour and style of the set.

Looking at this model, the lighting designer can plan where lamps should be placed.

Making a model

An important part of set design is making a scale model of the set. This gives the director, technicians and actors a chance to see what it will actually look like. They try to spot any construction problems or difficulties the actors might have with it before the real thing is actually built.

In a studio

There is no curtain to hide scene changes. Things must be moved by actors or stage hands.

A studio is usually a place where stage and seating can be moved to form unusual acting spaces. New sightlines must be worked out for each design. Studio work mostly has a small budget, so sets are often designed to be striking but relatively inexpensive.

A set in a claustrophobic corner might suit the mood of a play.

The floor is a focus, so its colour and texture are significant.

Audience

Set

Set

This cosy corner is made by rugs, cushions and warm lighting.

Actors can relate closely to the audience in this arrangement.

Audience

Props

Props, short for 'properties', are all the things needed to decorate the set and used by actors on stage. The props person has to make, hire*, borrow or buy them all. This must be done as cheaply as possible, so he must be ingenious and resourceful. He also takes care of props during the production, and stores or returns them all afterwards.

Dressing the set

Arranging all the props on stage and making sure the set looks right down to the last detail is known as dressing the set. The props person makes sure everything is in place and adds final touches for authenticity.

This is a sketch for a naturalistic set of a 19th century drawing room.

All props must be fireproofed.

The ornaments and decor reflect the status and tastes of the "owner".

Minimal props

Plain boxes can become chairs, tables, steps and so on.

Not all sets need realistic dressing. A low-budget or experimental production, or a play that demands a simple set, may involve very few props, used imaginatively.

Expensive things or ones that are hard to obtain can be faked (see page 25).

All furniture and fittings must be of the right period. They'd probably need to be hired.

Period colours and patterns must be researched in books and museums.

Personal props

An actor can use any props he carries on or wears during the play to help develop his role. For instance, a mannerism with a walking stick or fan can say a lot about the character. Sometimes the script specifies a prop, for example a pipe.

A wooden stick and a silver-topped cane make very different impressions.

Spectacles must suit the era and character.

Key props

Some props are crucial to the plot, such as glasses and drinks for a party scene, a significant letter to be delivered or a murder weapon in a thriller.

24

*rent (U.S.)

Faking it

Large, awkward or expensive props can usually be faked. Skilled props people fake props in ingenious ways, by making or adapting things from cheap materials. These are very convincing if they are only for show, not to be used.

Papier mâché

Papier mâché is a mush of torn paper and glue that dries hard. When wet, strips of it can be moulded in layers over a base to build up a solid shape.

This papier mâché bust of Shakespeare has a chicken wire base.

A balloon base can be popped when the papier mâché is dry, leaving a hollow, round shape.

Lumps, dried and painted, can be used as large, decorative jewels.

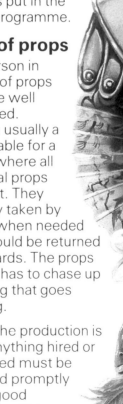

Polystyrene

As it is light and easy to carve, polystyrene is good for faking props that would be too heavy or awkward otherwise.

The basic shape is cut. Then papier mâché or material soaked in glue can be put on to add texture. It is painted when dry.

An old tombstone like this could be made by this method.

Everyday things

Ordinary, everyday things such as straws, paper doilies and string can all be added to plain things and painted to make them look rich and elaborate.

String wound round a plain vase, then painted gold.

String-covered piece of wood makes a sword handle.

Straws add "panels" to a plywood box.

Spraying paint through a doiley makes a fancy pattern.

String glued to a book and painted to make it look old and hand-bound.

Beg, borrow or buy

A prop that will be handled and used, not just seen, must usually be genuine and has to be bought, hired or borrowed. Props people learn to seek out junk shops and raid the attics and cellars of the cast and their friends to find things they need. Hiring is costly but may be the only source of more obscure things. Local shops and businesses will often lend things if their name is put in the play's programme.

Care of props

The person in charge of props must be well organized. There's usually a props table for a show, where all personal props are kept. They are only taken by actors when needed and should be returned afterwards. The props person has to chase up anything that goes missing.

When the production is over, anything hired or borrowed must be returned promptly and in good condition. Things bought or made become part of the company's permanent properties.

25

Costume

Costumes are part of the overall design of a production. They complete the impression of a historical period made by the set; influence the way actors feel and move; and their colour and texture help create the mood of the play.

The wardrobe

A theatre company's collection of costumes is called its wardrobe. The person in charge makes, buys or hires all the costumes for the company's productions. She is expert at buying material and trimmings cheaply, making "finds" at sales and seeing uses for unlikely bits and pieces.

Costume design

The costume designer discusses with the director the era the play is set in, or the style he wants to establish, and they decide together what outfit is best for each role. The designer then researches suitable styles in books, museums, paintings of the period and so on.

Next, the designer presents his visual ideas, along with thoughts on fabrics that might be used. Not all costume designers can draw, but they can show what they intend in other ways, such as collage from magazine clippings.

Men's beards and moustaches must be right, too.

Hair

Hair is just as important as clothes. Styles must be exactly right for a historical period or a character's personality. Back views have to be researched – paintings, photographs and even statues can help. Period wigs can be bought or hired, or cheap wigs styled to suit.

Painted nuts, bolts, beans, corks, pasta and so on can make effective, bulky jewellery.

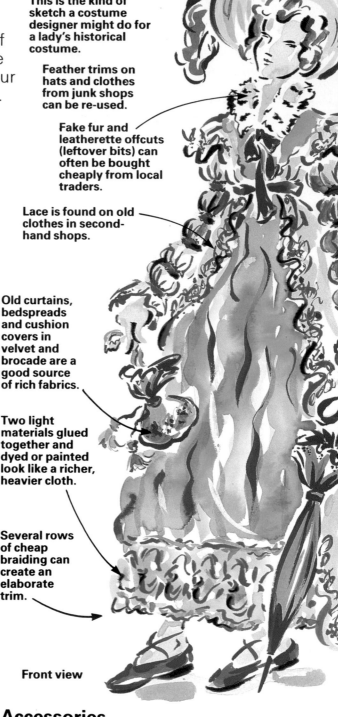

This is the kind of sketch a costume designer might do for a lady's historical costume.

Feather trims on hats and clothes from junk shops can be re-used.

Fake fur and leatherette offcuts (leftover bits) can often be bought cheaply from local traders.

Lace is found on old clothes in second-hand shops.

Old curtains, bedspreads and cushion covers in velvet and brocade are a good source of rich fabrics.

Two light materials glued together and dyed or painted look like a richer, heavier cloth.

Several rows of cheap braiding can create an elaborate trim.

Front view

Accessories

Accessories, such as jewellery, gloves, hats, shoes and so on add the finishing touches and make a real difference. Many can be made from cheap materials or adapted from modern things, with ingenuity. Particularly tricky items may have to be hired.

Making costumes

You need detailed measurements before you start on a costume, and it must be carefully fitted on the actor before it is finalized. Modern styles and simple shapes are the easiest to make.

Extra doodles show details.

This Roman style is made of cheap, white sheeting.

You need a historical pattern book for authentic period styles.

Pattern

19th century lady's dress

Adapting clothes

Modern clothes, bought cheaply in markets, can be adapted to other styles. A low-waisted dress can easily be turned into a 1920s style, for example.

Sleeves cut out

Floppy sash added

Hem altered

Underwear

Underwear affects the shape of outer garments and how the wearer moves in them, so period underclothes are vital.

A hooped crinoline goes under a 19th century dress.

A corset makes a distinctive silhouette.

Back view

Different colours were popular at certain times in history. Dyeing can create the right shades.

Breaking down

Making new clothes look old is called breaking them down. The cloth is scrubbed and dirtied in places it would wear naturally. A cheesegrater breaks the surface of the material well.

Collar

Elbows

Cuffs

Keeping costumes

Costumes should always be well cared for, hung up after each performance and washed or cleaned carefully according to what they are made of. Hired and borrowed costumes must be returned punctually. Bought and made items can be stored to adapt and use again.

Costume hung up and covered by a plastic bag. A label says which character it belongs to.

Make-up

In the past, stage make-up tended to be exaggerated, since theatre lights did not illuminate actors' faces well. Today, the least that is needed to make an actor look his best is all that is used, especially in a small venue. Heavier make-up is used to create special effects, for period make-up styles or to change the age of an actor.

Putting on make-up

It is usually only in film or television work that professional make-up artistes are available.

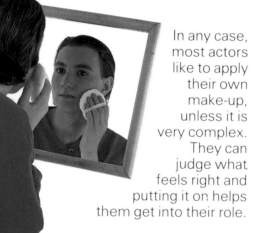

In any case, most actors like to apply their own make-up, unless it is very complex. They can judge what feels right and putting it on helps them get into their role.

Basic kit

There is a huge variety of theatrical make-up and actors have to try different types and brands to find which they prefer. Here are some of the things that are used. You can see how make-up is applied above.

Greasepaint is oil-based make-up. It comes hard in sticks, or softer in tubes, in a huge variety of colours. You put it on with your fingers.

You need tissues and so on for removing make-up.

Cake make-up comes in blocks and is put on with a damp sponge.

Straight make-up

A "straight" make-up just enhances the features. Here's how it is done.
- A base colour to match the skin is evenly spread on. Concealer goes on blemishes.
- Dark brown is blended under the chin, along the jaw line, down the sides of the nose and above the eyebrows to give shape back to the face.
- Pale highlighter on cheekbones, brow bones, upper lip, above the jaw bone and down the centre of the nose emphasizes the parts that protrude.
- Rouge adds warmth along the cheekbones and the centre of forehead and chin.
- The eye is outlined with dark brown pencil.
- Translucent powder, patted on, sets the make-up.
- Eyeshadow is used to define the eyes. Men use a neutral colour. Women may match their eyes or outfit and add mascara.
- Eyes are highlighted with white powder under the eyebrow and in the inner corner.

- Lips are outlined with lip pencil then filled in with red. Men, or women for a natural look, use colours close to their lip shade.
- The final effect is dusted with blending powder.

Make-up must be applied in front of a well-lit mirror.

Make-up removing cream

Box with lid to keep make-up tidily.

Blending powder smooths and evens out make-up and prevents greasepaint shining.

Fine brushes for applying details.

Colour sticks for eyes and lips.

Rouge

Sponges

Changing faces

All sorts of dramatic changes can be made with make-up. Here are two examples.

The face on the left shows how the make-up is applied. This photograph shows the result.

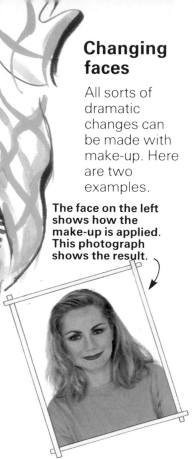

This is the actor before any make-up is put on. Look at his face closely.

Now shading and highlighter are used to change the shape of his nose.

Stubble, applied with a sponge, and greased hair make him look disreputable.

This blonde, fresh-faced girl is going to get a strange, fantasy make-up.

Her skin is tinted unnaturally pale. Her eyes and brows are dramatized.

Scarlet lips and a new hair-do and colour make her almost unrecognizable.

Ageing make-up

• A pale, sallow base is used.
• Natural age lines on the forehead and around the eyes, cheeks and mouth are found by making exaggerated expressions and marking the lines with a dark pencil.
• The eyes are made to sink in by filling the lids and under the eyes with dark brown. Dark brown also goes under the chin.
• Highlighter goes along the upper side of all the wrinkles and the centre of the nose.
• Mid-brown powder shades the hollows in the cheeks, temples and sides of the nose.
• Brows are made bushier with grey and white mascara.
• Lips are pale and narrow. Thin streaks of alternate crimson and ivory around them make pucker lines.

Here is the finished effect. Once the colours are blended it is convincing from quite close-to.

• Grey mascara tints eyelashes. Talc and white mascara make the hair grey.
• Translucent powder all over sets the make-up.
• The neck and hands should be aged, too.

29

Lighting

Lighting in theatres is very special. Usually, the main lights in the theatre, called house lights, dim when a performance is about to start. Then the stage lights come on, creating a mood of anticipation as the show begins.

Kinds of lamps

Theatre lights are usually called lanterns or lamps, from the old days when they were gas or oil. Today, they can be very powerful, sometimes up to 2,000 Watts (the bulbs you use are mostly 60-100 Watts). There are many different kinds of lamps. These are the main ones.

Flood lamps

Flood lamps spread an even flood of light over the stage.

This is a batten. It is a row of flood lamps used to give a broad spread of light on the cyclorama (see page 21).

(see page 21)

Profile spot

Spotlights can be directed at specific areas. A profile spot has a hard-edged beam, shaped by moving shutters on each side of the lens.

Slides put in a slot in front of the lens can alter the shape of the beam.

Fresnel spot

This spotlight has a softer-edged beam, used for general lighting.

Modifying the lamps

Most lamps can be modified to change the shape, colour or quality of their light.

Coloured filters called gels can be put in front of the lens. ▼

Gobos are sheets of aluminium with holes cut in them, put in front of the lens to make shapes. ▼

Barn-doors shape the beam and cut out "spill" (unwanted light). ▼

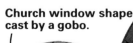

Colour adds a lot to the mood of the light.

Church window shape cast by a gobo.

Barn-doors

How the lamps work

Lamps can be controlled by manual systems, such as this one, or by computer. It helps to know how the manual system works, in any case.

Dimmer packs

Wires from lamps are first plugged into a dimmer pack. This is a box with special circuits that can alter the flow of power to a lamp to make it brighter or dimmer.

This pack has six dimmer circuits with two sockets each. Lamps on the same dimmer are "paired". They go on and off together. ➤

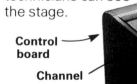

The combined power of lamps on one dimmer must not exceed 2,000 Watts. ➤

The control board

Each dimmer is connected to a channel on the control board. This is often in a soundproofed room behind the audience, from where the technicians can see the stage.

Control board ➤

Channel ➤

Each channel controls lights from one dimmer circuit.

Faders

A sliding knob, or fader, on each channel makes the dimmer brighten or dim the lamps. 10 is bright, 1 is dim and 0 is off.

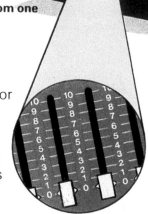

Lighting design

For a good basic design, the designer creates a balanced light that looks natural and avoids awkward shadows. It should enhance the textures of costumes and scenery and help make objects and actors three-dimensional. To achieve this, he uses a combination of lamps, shone from three main places: the front, sides and back of the stage.

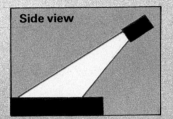

Front lighting covers the stage well but, on its own, makes things look flat and boring.

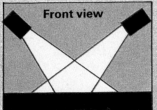

Side-lighting, at an angle of 45°, imitates daylight and casts natural shadows.

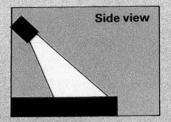

Back lighting outlines people and objects and makes them stand out from the scenery.

Top lighting helps cut out shadows and highlights colours and textures.

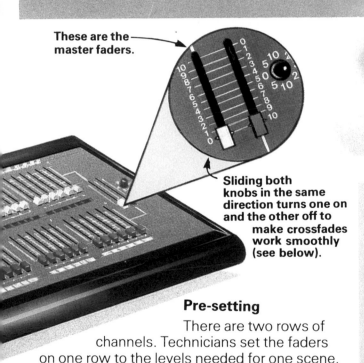

These are the master faders.

Sliding both knobs in the same direction turns one on and the other off to make crossfades work smoothly (see below).

Pre-setting

There are two rows of channels. Technicians set the faders on one row to the levels needed for one scene. The second row is set to the levels for the next scene. This is called pre-setting.

Crossfade

All the channels on one row are worked by a master fader. To change from one pre-set to another, you slide one master fader on and the other off. Done smoothly and slowly, this is called a crossfade. When the master fader is off, faders can be moved without changing the lights, so a new pre-set can be prepared.

Special effects

Once an overall light is achieved, extra lamps may be added for effect, such as one with a bluish gel for moonlight, or a clouds gobo.

Any lighting angle on its own makes a special effect, too. Top light casts weird shadows on faces and back light gives an eerie silhouette.

The designer's job

Good lighting makes the very best of costumes and set. Bad lighting can spoil the whole effect. The designer must liaise with all the other people involved in styling the play to see what mood is being created. Then he makes a plan on paper, using symbols to show where the lamps will be hung. He also supervises the hanging and connecting of lamps.

In performance, the Deputy Stage Manager (see page 35) follows the play and tells the lighting technicians when a change is due.

A signal for when the lights change is called a cue. A cue sheet reminds technicians exactly what change is required.

Lighting plan

PAGE	CUE	DESCRIPTION	TIME
		crossfade	5 sec.
		rout.	3 sec.
		ild	60 sec
		ION.	15 sec.	4
		ging	35 sec	5

Sound

In the theatre there is no natural background noise, as in films and television. Any sounds or music needed to evoke atmosphere must be consciously chosen and made during the show. Some noises, such as a crack of thunder, may be an important part of the script. In a musical show, singers and musicians must be heard clearly as they sing or play.

Producing different sounds

Sounds are called "live" if they are made during the performance, such as someone singing.

Pre-recorded sounds are made on a tape and played back at the right moment.

Microphones are placed in the theatre to pick up live sounds.

You can buy sound effects cassettes, records and CDs with noises such as pouring rain, or a car on gravel on them.

Music played on record, cassette or compact disc may be relayed into the auditorium.

The sound crew must use their initiative. They may need to go somewhere unusual to record a particular effect live; sometimes they dub several sounds together to make an unusual effect; or "cheat" by imitating a sound.

A thin sheet of metal made to wobble sounds convincingly like a grumble of thunder. The more it wobbles, the louder the sound.

Broadcasting sounds

Whether a sound is pre-recorded or live it must be amplified and broadcast so that all the audience can hear it. This is how it is usually done.

Pre-recorded sounds are recorded onto a tape, in the sequence in which they will be needed.

Reel-to-reel recorder

A reel-to-reel recorder is used rather than a cassette because the sound crew needs to be able to get at the tape. Find out why, and how the tape is made, below.

A theatre usually has a turntable, cassette player and CD player. They produce sounds or music to be recorded onto the main tape. Sometimes, effects are broadcast direct from them.

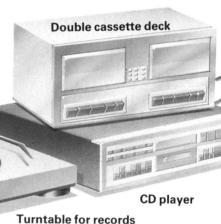

Double cassette deck

CD player

Turntable for records

Making an effects tape

The sounds are recorded onto one tape. Then the tape is spliced. This means that lengths of tape, each with a single sound on, are sliced off, then re-joined in the right order with marker tape between them. Machines can do this, but this is a simple manual method.

The tape is laid in a groove in a wooden splicing block and cut diagonally with a sharp blade.

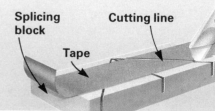

Splicing block

Cutting line

Tape

The sound crew

The sound crew discuss all the effects needed in the play with the director. Then they prepare them and make a sound tape if necessary. During the performance, they sit in the technical box with the lighting technicians and operate the sound equipment. As for lighting, in professional theatres the cues for sound effects are read by the Deputy Stage Manager (see page 35).

A sound cue sheet lists the sounds, describes them and says how long each should last.

View of the stage from the technical box.

All these sound sources are plugged into a machine called a mixer. This controls which sound is heard and how loud it is. It can fade sounds in and out, too.

The mixer is plugged into an amplifier, which makes noises louder.

Amplifier

Microphones

Mixer

Portable speaker

The sound from the amplifier is broadcast through speakers. For balance, there is usually a speaker on each side of the stage. Small, portable speakers are used if a sound has to come from a specific direction.

Speaker

A piece of special magnetic tape is fastened to the end of each section of sound effects tape. This automatically stops the recorder playing, so it does not run on to the next sound.

A piece of tape called leader tape is fixed to the other end of the magnetic tape. The free end of the leader tape is then joined to the next bit of the sound effects tape.

Sound tape

Leader tape

Magnetic tape

Sound tape

Different-coloured leader tape can be used to identify each effect.

This is repeated until the whole tape is joined together again.

The director: planning and rehearsing a play

Although a play seems spontaneous, it is really carefully planned and rehearsed. It is the director's job to bring all the elements together smoothly. This is very hard work but is also extremely exciting and rewarding.

Countdown

Here you can get some idea of the many things that have to be done in the build-up to a show. Professionals may have to do it all in a few weeks. Amateurs only work in their spare time and would have to plan a much longer schedule.

First things first

Before work starts, the director must decide basic things about the production.

He collects ideas for costumes and sets, and thinks about the lighting and acting style.

He holds meetings with everyone involved in making and designing costumes and sets, to discuss his ideas and the budgets and deadlines.

He plans what sort of auditions will help him find the kinds of actors he needs.

The rehearsal schedule is planned and typed up ready to give to the actors.

The rehearsal schedule must be realistic, according to how much time is available.

Getting going

The director holds auditions. He may ask actors to prepare speeches from the play, or to improvise together to see how they respond. He chooses his actors and hands out scripts and rehearsal schedules. At a first read-through, actors read the play aloud together.

First rehearsals

Rehearsals begin, usually in a rehearsal room rather than on stage. At first there is detailed work on single scenes or short sections. Actors work with their scripts in hand. The set design is agreed so the set builders can get going.

Amateurs have to work on their own publicity, too.

Later rehearsals

At later rehearsals, everyone should know their lines and the director concentrates on getting the best performances from the actors (see next page). The director now fixes the blocking of the play. Find out what this means on the right.

Finishing touches

Close to performance, the director has regular meetings with everyone to make sure all is on schedule. The final lighting design is approved.

Set, costumes and props are approved. Equipment is hired.

As soon as it's practical, rehearsals move onto the real stage and take the form of run-throughs – whole acts rehearsed in one go. The director does not interrupt. He notes any problems to discuss with people afterwards.

The final days

The last days before a show go something like this:
Day 4: put up set; rig lights.
Day 3: technical rehearsal to make sure all light and sound effects work. Actors in full costume go through the play, sometimes skipping between technical cues. It can be boring for the actors but is vital to the smooth running of the show.
Day 2: final rehearsals. Then dress rehearsal, performing the whole play as if for real.
Day 1: second dress rehearsal.

First night

The first night is nerve-wracking and thrilling. The director makes more notes in order to fine-tune the performance afterwards.

REHEARSALS

Mon 7
7.30pm   Act 1
                Sc. 3

Wed
7.30pm   Act 1
                Sc

Fri 11   Dolly
7   Cl

Working with actors

This is the most demanding and rewarding thing the director does. He usually has a fairly clear idea of how he wants characters to develop, but he cannot dictate to actors. He must let them explore their own feelings, talk to them, make suggestions and coax the performance he wants from them.

From a distance the director sees the impact various groupings and movements will have on an audience.

Actors often stop and ask the director's opinion about how to deliver a line.

A director must be aware of all the different techniques that can be used in rehearsal (some are discussed on pages 14-15) and choose ones that encourage the acting style he wants. The director's most important role is to be outside the action and judge objectively how it comes across and if it could be improved.

Blocking

Blocking means deciding where and when characters will move on stage. At first, the director has general ideas about where a scene will take place (some moves are written in the stage directions or are obvious from the words). More precise positions are decided by what feels and looks right to the director and actors, and what makes sense for the characters.

The director must also consider the set design. It may give him new ideas for blocking, and its shape will decide which areas are best for the main action to take place in. The sightlines (see page 22) must be worked out and taken into account.

Blocking is only fixed towards the end of rehearsal time.

The stage management team

The stage manager (SM) oversees all that happens during preparation for a performance, such as gathering props and building the set, to make sure it is going according to plan. During the performance, she takes charge backstage and makes sure that the set, props and actors are ready and in the right place.

The deputy stage manager (DSM) keeps a "book", which is the bible for running the show. She attends meetings with technical staff and goes to rehearsals to note down any changes the director requires. She tells the stage manager, who makes sure they get done.

During performances, the DSM sits in the technical box, using the book to give cues for sound and lighting effects and, if necessary, for an actor's entrance.

All information about the play is kept in the DSM's book.

The book is a loose-leaf file. The play script is cut up and put in it. Paper is put between each page for writing all the notes on.

1) B DS→D (in doorway)
2) D XS→SL (as script)
3) As script
4) R XS→CSL As script
5) As Script (B moves across R)
6) B exits SL to car park

CALL MR MASON

These are all the blocking moves and so on.

Assistant stage managers (ASMs) help the stage manager.

Planning a musical

Musicals are tremendously popular. Spectacular professional productions cost lots of money and attract large audiences. Amateurs like doing them, too, as there are so many enjoyable ways to take part.

Chorus further forward.

right!

The creative team

The director co-ordinates the whole creative team. She is responsible for the final look, pace and impact of the show. To produce a musical, she needs even more help than for a play.

The director has to keep tabs on every aspect of the performance.

The musical director may write original music or use an existing score.

This Labanotation (code for dance) was invented by Laban (page 4).

First, the director must find a good musical director to teach the actors their songs, inspire enthusiastic renderings of them and hire suitable musicians to play.

She also needs a choreographer to devise and teach dance routines. The choreographer has to deal with group dances for a chorus and solo routines for the stars.

Auditions

Actors in musicals usually have to sing and dance as well as act, so auditions take much longer.

Musicals succeed or fail on how well their songs are put across. A good song, badly sung, is a disaster. A weak song done well can get by. At audition, an actor may sing a song of his choice, then one from the show.

In dance auditions, the choreographer looks for well-trained dancers with ability, rhythm and style.

Much of the acting of a musical role comes across through dancing and singing, so the director attends all the auditions to see how actors come across. She may do more acting tests to make sure of their ability.

Rehearsals

These follow a different pattern to play rehearsals and take a longer time to complete.

The first weeks

The actors learn the songs first so the musical director is in charge during the early weeks.

The director is often there to advise how the songs should be sung to suit the role.

The choreographer may come along to judge how complex she can make her dances while still leaving the actors enough breath to sing.

The next steps

Choreography comes next. The dances are based on the rhythms of the songs.

The director watches so that she can help to find ways of linking the spoken sections smoothly with the songs and dances.

She also wants to see that the choreography uses the set to its full potential.

Costumes

Costumes in musicals are often bright and glamorous. Their main purpose is not to be realistic but to bring a strong, attractive theme or style to the show. The director must check with the costume designer that actors will be able to sing and dance easily in their costumes.

The dancers in this chorus are wearing costumes linked by a bright colour scheme.

Other elements

Here are some of the added problems that the backstage and technical staff on a musical must think about.

● Sound engineers must wire microphones over the stage to pick up live singing.
● The theatre's acoustics must be tested to see where it is best for musicians to sit.
● There is often complex lighting, used to evoke moods and complement dance styles.
● What the stage is made of is important. It must not echo or creak to spoil the rhythm and effect of dances.
● The set must be extra strong as it should not wobble or shake with the energetic pounding it will get from the dancers.

Stress and strain

Musicals are physically very demanding. It's easy to pull a muscle or strain your voice, so warming-up and relaxing are especially important.

Even a cold can put a performer out of action. Understudies are actors who learn another part that they could take over at any time.

They often already have a small role in the show, but get the chance to understudy a larger one.

You will usually see an insert like this in the programme if an understudy is to play a part.

Due to illness, the part of Aunt Agnes will be played by Joan Walsh tonight.

Uniting the whole

When the director finally takes over, much of what will happen on stage is already fixed by the singing and dancing. She then works on blending all the elements into a slick, stylish show.

The musicians do not take part until right at the end. For rehearsals, usually just a piano is needed. It costs too much to pay musicians to rehearse and, in any case, it is best to concentrate on one thing at a time while people are learning.

Story lines

Because of the cost, musicals have to be sure-fire successes. That's why they tend to stick to well-tried stories, themes and musical styles.

Amateur groups can enliven a show by adapting it to their audience. Slipping in references to or jokes about local people or events can make it a big hit.

Acting in films and television

The same basic skills are needed for all acting, but there are many differences between theatre work and films or television. Instead of a live audience, actors perform in front of cameras which record them on film or video tape. This affects every aspect of their work.

How a film is made

Filming is called "shooting". It is very expensive as it involves sophisticated equipment, lots of skilled people and going to different places, or locations, to shoot.

Episodes in a film are often shot in the wrong order. It is cheaper to shoot all the scenes in one location at the same time, even if they do not follow on directly in the film's story, or screenplay.

Scenes that do follow each other may be shot weeks apart. A continuity person makes sure that the actors' hair, costumes and other details match up in consecutive scenes.

When the shooting is over, post-production starts. The director and film editor put the scenes in order and cut out parts they do not want. This is done in a similar way to splicing a sound tape (page 32) and is called editing.

The director's influence

A theatre director works closely with the actors right up to performance, then he hands over to them. A film director has control before, during and after filming. The camera angles and shots he chooses (see below), which scenes he uses and which he cuts, and even how he splices scenes together, alter how the audience understands the film. The producer who finances the film also has influence. For example, he may insist on a different ending because he thinks it will be more popular.

Vista shots

A vista scene is shot from far away, to give a sense of place. No-one knows what is important in it.

Long shots

These are still shot from quite far away, but you begin to pick out part of the scene to focus on.

Medium shots

These bring you closer to the focus of the scene. You start to see exactly what is happening.

Close-ups

The camera closes in on an expression or detail that the director particularly wants you to notice.

The director can also shoot from unusual angles, or show something else on screen while an actor is speaking, for example. An actor often does not know exactly how the director is framing the scene while he is performing it.

How film actors work

Shooting a scene in a film is called "doing a take". Actors often have little or no rehearsal time, since if a take goes wrong, they can usually film it again. Paying actors to rehearse would cost more, so film actors mostly prepare alone.

Film actors must concentrate hard. As well as working with other actors, they have to aim their performance at specific cameras and work around filming equipment and crew without colliding.

Even intimate moments in the film are shot with machinery and people all around.

Acting must be very precise, especially in medium shot or close-up. The camera picks up every blink or twitch.

Actors have to make moves accurately, since they must be in the right place within centimetres for a camera to get the required shot. Positions are marked with tape on the floor.

A lot of patience is needed on a film set. Actors often have nothing to do while the director and technicians prepare. Then they must be ready to perform even the most emotional scene after a long and boring wait.

Method acting

Because of the way films are shot, actors rarely work towards a single, continuous performance, as in the theatre.

Since films generally demand naturalistic, understated acting and the ability to slip into a role at any stage in the screenplay, many actors find it helps to be completely immersed in their part so that they can "become" their character in an instant.

These are some American film stars and actors trained in the Method.

Marlon Brando

Marilyn Monroe

Robert De Niro

Al Pacino.

Method acting is a way of training to do this. It is an intensely life-like acting style developed by the American, Lee Strasberg. Based on Stanislavsky's system (see next page), it trains actors to identify with their roles and give a spontaneous, emotional performance.

Acting in television

Television performances require much of the same patience and accuracy as for film. Television is usually shot on video tape. This can be edited, like film, but TV productions tend to have smaller budgets, so actors may work more as in the theatre, with a short rehearsal period followed by continuous filming of scenes in sequence.

Many television comedy series, called situation comedies, or sitcoms, are recorded in as continuous a way as possible. There is often a live audience, and this helps get, and record, a natural response from them. Many directors and producers believe this makes the show more appealing.

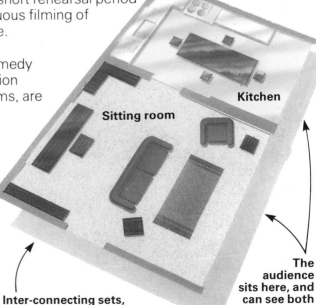

Kitchen

Sitting room

The audience sits here, and can see both rooms.

Inter-connecting sets, like this one, allow the action to move from room to room without stopping.

Sets that appear each week in a sitcom may be set up permanently for recording.

39

Stanislavsky: a new style

Some individuals have been so influential that they have changed the whole of theatrical thinking. The Russian director, Konstantin Stanislavsky, was one of these. He started work in the theatre towards the end of the 19th Century. At that time, in commercial European theatre, little time was given to rehearsals or directing. Stock sets and costumes were used whatever the play and star actors dominated productions. Actors tended to play types, rather than developing individual roles and their style was exaggerated and melodramatic.

The system

Stanislavsky was dissatisfied with this. In 1898 he set up his own company, the Moscow Arts Theatre. There, he gradually developed an approach to acting that is sometimes called his "system", though his beliefs were not fixed, but changed and progressed. His work had a huge influence on the growth of a more natural acting style and the development of the crucial role of the director in modern theatre.

Finding the truth

Stanislavsky wanted actors to think deeply about their roles, and make them true-to-life. Here are some of the ways he got actors to do this.

An actor studies her part and slowly feels her way into it, using Stanislavsky's methods.

Psychological truth

He looked for performances that sprang from an understanding of the inner feelings and motives of a character, or its psychological truth. He believed actors would only know how to move and speak if they understood how a character thought and felt.

If I was poor and freezing, I'd be as wretched as I was at that match last winter.

In order to act being cold, this actor remembers a time when he was freezing.

The magic "if"

Actors could not always have lived through the experiences of characters in a play. Stanislavsky encouraged them to recall if they had felt anything similar and to remember what it was like. He told them to say, "If I was this person, in this situation, how would I feel and what would I do?" He called this the magic "if".

The given circumstances

The actor had to discover the purpose of every speech and action by his character. He looked for clues in the play: everything the character said or did, what was said about him, stage directions describing his home, possessions, habits or appearance. These were called the given circumstances.

Working with given circumstances today

For Stanislavsky, the given circumstances were only drawn from the text of the play. Today, a director may allow actors to use their imaginations to deepen their understanding of what is in the text through hot-seating (page 14), impro (pages 12-13) or exercises such as writing a diary for the character.

Things that happened in the play are written up from the character's point of view in the diary.

It can also include imagined details of his daily life.

August 9th
Called to se
he was n
need th
felt s

Breaking down the play

In order to understand the play and each role in it, Stanislavsky insisted on dissecting it and looking at each part in detail. This is how he did it.

Units

The play was broken into small units to study. A unit could be as short as a couple of lines, or as long as a whole scene.

One unit was about the same subject or developed an idea. A new character entering might start a new unit, for example.

Intentions

Each speech in a unit was examined to work out why the character said it and what he hoped to achieve by it (his intention). Sometimes, to decide on the intention, a character's overall motivation in the scene had to be understood (see below).

Intentions are not always obvious.

A character may speak warmly to one person in order to make another feel unwanted or left out, for example.

In this case, what he is saying and how he says it do not tell you directly what his intention is.

A speech might not at first seem to suit the character's objective, but must prove to do so in the end.

Being unusually friendly as a build up to asking for money would be one example of this.

Objectives

The aim of a character in any scene was called his objective. Everything he said and did contributed to it. Anything that did not fit in either had to be seen another way, or the actor had to re-think his objective.

Through-line

A character's objectives in every scene added up to his through-line, or main purpose in the play. Often there is a key speech that sums this up, which the actor can keep in mind as he plays the part.

The superobjective

When all the actors had worked out their through-lines, they decided together on a superobjective for the whole play. This meant the main thing it was trying to show or tell us about the characters and the situation they were in.

Stanislavsky and staging

At the Moscow Arts Theatre, Stanislavsky tried to make his productions as authentic as he could. If the play involved people or places that really existed, he arranged for his actors to study or visit them to help fire their imaginations. A lot of effort was put into making sets and costumes look as real as possible.

Natural style today

Today, a play performed in Stanislavsky's style would not seem particularly naturalistic to theatre audiences, although this was so revolutionary at the time. Today's audience is used to the realism of film and television productions (read more on pages 38-39) and does not expect theatre to try to reproduce it. This has led many directors and theatre companies to explore other styles of work and ask what it is that theatre can offer which television and film cannot.

Brecht and the epic theatre

After Stanislavsky, most European theatres aimed for a naturalistic style. It took another original figure to challenge this way of performing. Bertolt Brecht was a German playwright and director whose work became another major influence on 20th century drama. You can read about some of his theories below.

Political theatre

Brecht began writing plays in 1918, and directing in 1922. He believed that most drama at that time was passive. Comfortable in a warm, dark theatre, all the audience did was watch. They might sympathize with what they saw, but could only accept it as inevitable.

Brecht thought this was wrong. He wanted audiences to be wide awake and critical.

In 1926, Brecht began to study the political and economic theories of Karl Marx. Marx said that working people would revolt and take power from the wealthy few for the benefit of everybody.

Brecht became convinced that theatre should be political as well as entertaining. He wanted people to react when they saw injustice or suffering on stage and leave determined to change it.

Karl Marx expounded his theories in several books, including Das Kapital.

The epic style

To make political theatre, Brecht developed what he called an epic style. His plays, the acting style he encouraged and his staging ideas all contributed to it.

An epic play is one that tells a story as a sequence of events rather than concentrating on an individual's feelings and thoughts.

In this way, an epic play shows historical changes, concentrating upon the practical effects of one person's actions upon another.

On the right are listed some of the best-known plays Brecht wrote in his epic style:

The Threepenny Opera 1929-31

St. Joan of the Stockyards 1929-31

Mother Courage and her Children 1941

The Life of Galileo 1943

The Good Person of Szechwan 1943

The Caucasian Chalk Circle 1954

Brecht and actors

Brecht did not want actors to relate to roles in the same way as Stanislavsky, but to act as if showing the story of what their characters had done. Here are some exercises Brecht used in rehearsals.

Actors said their words as reported speech, as if they were said by someone else.

This is the line in the play.

"What do you want?" she asked.

The actor adds this to make reported speech.

To make the actors feel they were telling a story rather than "living" it, they said aloud what their characters did as well as said.

Staging

Brecht wanted to keep people alert so they would be critical of characters rather than sympathizing with them. Here are some of the ways he broke the illusion of the theatre.

● Bright lights showed up the wiring and scenery for what it was so people did not forget where they were. House lights were not turned off.

● Some of Brecht's plays had narrator characters to comment on and link scenes.

● Many of Brecht's plays had songs in the middle of scenes. These often took a different view of the action, for contrast.

All these things disrupted the flow of the story and made the audience look at it from different angles.

● Actors might sit on stage even when they were not in a scene. They did not pretend to stay in character, but became spectators.

● Actors frequently played more than one role in a play so the audience did not associate them with one part.

● Captions projected on screens also commented on the action.

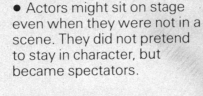

The alienation effect

Brecht used the term alienation for a moment in a play when the audience sees a familiar thing as strange.

It was meant to prevent people taking things for granted and make them realize that things could change if they had the political will.

Brecht's staging ideas helped bring about alienation. This did not mean insulting or offending the audience.

Brecht in exile

Because of his political views, Brecht left Germany in 1933, as the Nazi Party came to power. He lived in Europe and America and wrote many of his best-known plays at this time. He returned to Germany in 1948 and in 1949 set up the Berlin Ensemble theatre company. He died in 1956.

Enter Shirley. Jane: Are you still here?

This is what is in the script.

Shirley entered the room and looked around.

Actor playing Shirley.

"Are you still here?" said Jane standing up.

Actor playing Jane.

This is the line in the play. →

Smith (to Walker): Sit down.

He didn't tell Walker to leave the room, he told him to sit down. "Sit down," he said.

Actor playing Smith. →

As he acts, it is as if he says to the audience "This character did this but he could have done that instead".

To prevent audiences thinking actions were inevitable, Brecht wanted to make it clear that a play only showed one version of events. He made actors aware of this by making them say what characters did not do as well as what they did.

Brecht hoped people would see the possibility of political change if they understood that things happened because of the choices people made.

The history of European theatre

From the earliest times, people have acted out crucial rituals and events in their lives. Later, special places were built for performances and acting as a skilled profession began. Theatre buildings, styles of acting and people's opinion of drama have varied through history and in different parts of the world.

The Ancient Greeks

Drama in Europe first grew out of religious festivals in honour of the Ancient Greek god, Dionysus. They were held once a year and every citizen was expected to attend. Acting out stories about the gods helped to reinforce their religious beliefs.

Festivals were held in amphitheatres, which were the first permanent theatre buildings. They seated up to 20,000 people, the whole population of a city and its surroundings.

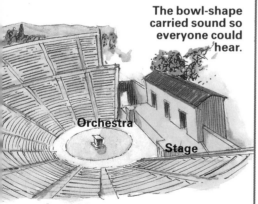

The bowl-shape carried sound so everyone could hear.

Orchestra

Stage

Amphitheatres were built into steeply sloping ground.

The audience sat on benches, looking down.

Actors were larger than life in padded costumes, masks and built-up shoes. They acted in a stylized way.

This is an Ancient carving of a Greek comic mask.

Classic Greek drama usually featured three actors who performed individual roles on the raised stage. A group of fifteen actors, called the Chorus, stood in the Orchestra. They helped tell the story, linked scenes together, commented on the play and were a vital part of the performance. All the actors were men.

The best-known Ancient Greek playwrights are Aeschylus, Aristophanes and Euripides (see Who's Who).

Aristotle

The first theory of drama was developed by an Ancient Greek philosopher called Aristotle. His writings have had a huge influence on theatre ever since. In his work, *Poetics*, he defined theatre, its purpose and many aspects of dramatic performance in terms that are still used today.

Some Aristotelian terms

Nemesis: a moment of human weakness that begins a character's downfall.

Catharsis: the purging you feel when watching tragedy.

Unities of action, time and place: the idea that a tragedy should consist of one main action, taking place within 24 hours in a single place. This influential theory is associated with Aristotle, although he only actually insisted on the unity of action.

The Romans

Roman theatre derived from Greek drama. It was also performed at festivals, but these tended to be celebrations of human wealth and power rather than religious ceremonies.

Under the Romans, the action on the raised stage became more important than what the Chorus did, and the Chorus role began to disappear from their plays.

"Low-life" characters, such as servants, became popular and were a great source of comedy. All characters, but especially these comic ones, began not to wear masks. This allowed more character development and interaction between characters on stage.

The great Roman authors are Seneca and Plautus (see Who's Who).

The Romans built theatres wherever they went. Remains of them can still be seen all over what was their empire.

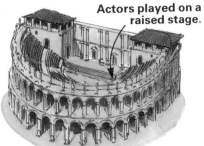

Actors played on a raised stage.

Roman theatres were built on flat ground, with surrounding walls.

As there was no Chorus, there was no need for an Orchestra.

Gradually, live theatre became extravagant, bawdy and disreputable. Spectacular events held in amphitheatres such as the Colosseum were disapproved of by the new Christian Romans who tried to discourage people from going.

Roman mosaic showing actors performing.

At last, theatre was banned on Sundays, then altogether. By the 6th century AD all theatres in Europe were closed.

Medieval theatre

Theatre skills were carried on by wandering performers, but theatre as such did not revive until the 10th century. Then, plays again began to be used in religious festivals to teach people the Bible stories. At first, they were performed inside churches, but they soon moved outside.

Each guild (group of craftsmen) acted out a Bible story to form a cycle. Plays were performed on wagons in churchyards or market squares.

The Bible stories were called Miracle Plays.

The devil was a popular figure in Miracle Plays.

Morality plays were also performed. They were stories of clear-cut Good and Evil with a moral ending.

Although the plays were religious, comedy parts were introduced and actors spoke their own language, not Latin, which was used in church. This meant that social and political issues crept into performances. For this reason, the church in the end disapproved of them.

16th century

Once again, theatres began to be built all over Europe. In England and Spain, the first ones were much like the inn yards where travelling performers had always played.

These were the kinds of theatres that Shakespeare's plays were performed in. The picture in the next column shows what they were like.

Open air theatres like this had no artificial light so performances were in the daytime.

This canopy was called the heavens.

Tiring house. Actors got changed here. Tiring was another word for attiring (getting dressed).

There was no scenery, except perhaps a basic background on the tiring house wall.

Platform for actors thrust into the centre of the courtyard.

The theatre held two to three thousand people. They stood in the galleries or courtyard.

Travelling groups of actors began to find rich, theatre-loving patrons to help them pay for places to perform, costumes and so on. Plays were also sometimes performed indoors, in nobles' houses or at the royal court.

People from all walks of life went to the theatre. Actors mainly wore contemporary clothes, regardless of where or when a play was set. In England, boys played female parts so there were no actresses, but women acted in France and other countries.

Commedia dell'Arte

Commedia dell'Arte is the name of a form of theatre, originally from Italy, that had an enormous influence on all European theatre. Commedia troupes were wandering players who improvised witty plays around a basic storyline. There were stock plots and characters, which relied on the actors' skill and ingenuity to bring them to life.

Hero and heroine

Stories usually featured the hero and heroine as young lovers trying to get together.

The heroine's grumpy father or guardian, Pantalone, tried to thwart the lovers.

Arlecchino

Colombina

Comic servants called zanni helped or hindered the pair.

Most Commedia figures wore leather masks so they traditionally expressed themselves in a very physical way with lots of acrobatics and slapstick comedy.

The influence of Commedia can be seen throughout the history of European comedy.

Arlecchino, Colombina and Pantalone became the characters Harlequin, Columbine and Pantaloon in 19th century English pantomime (see page 48).

Another zanni, called Pulcinella, was known as the comic figure Polichinelle in France, and in England as Punchinello. Punchinello then developed into Mr. Punch in Punch and Judy shows.

Punch and Judy shows are still traditional at the English seaside.

17th century

In France and Italy they did not build outdoor theatres. The Italians rediscovered the Greek Classics and realized that a new kind of stage was needed on which to perform them. Architects began to build indoor theatres and by 1600 had developed the proscenium arch style with sophisticated scenery which was soon copied throughout Europe.

The proscenium arch framed the stage and made it seem as though a picture created on the stage came to life.

Perspective scenery was created with flats and backdrops.

Banned

Developments in English theatre were halted by the Civil War. In 1642, all theatres were closed by Oliver Cromwell, the Puritan leader who came to power after defeating King Charles I. He felt that theatres bred immorality and dissent.

When Charles II was restored to the English throne in 1660, indoor theatres along Italian lines began to be built and English actresses appeared for the first time on stage.

Theatre flourished in the rest of Europe. In France, the comedies of Molière and tragedies of Racine were being performed and in Spain it was called the Golden Age, with plays by Calderón and Lope de Vega. There was no similar upsurge of theatre in Germany, mainly due to constant wars and religious troubles.

Theatre at this time was mainly a courtly activity and plays were written for well-educated, noble audiences.

18th century

In the 1700s, theatre-going was very fashionable. Playhouses were large and less intimate and the typical acting style became more mannered to suit. Books were even written about how to express emotions on stage.

Enthusiasm

Devotion

Horror

Distraction

Persuasion

Illustrations like these showed actors how to convey strong feelings.

In England, actor-managers such as David Garrick, who owned or ran their own theatre and acted in it, began to turn acting into the trained profession it is today.

Theatre was interrupted in France by the Revolution in 1789, but the lighter side of theatre was encouraged by Napoleon once he came to power.

German theatre began to develop, too. There were early attempts to perform historical plays in period costume and Goethe's theatrical masterpieces were being written and performed.

19th century

In the 19th century, very large theatres were built, seating as many as 3,500. Whole families would attend a noisy, spectacular night's entertainment.

Plays were accompanied by music, and the scale of the performance and special effects called for a vigorous, exaggerated acting style.

Melodrama was the most popular kind of play. Flamboyance and emotion were admired above all and the main aim was to move the audience. The leading actor was the centre of attention, and the best ones became stars whom people went especially to see.

Music Hall and Revue

In the second half of the century, shows offering huge bills of mixed acts, such as soliloquies (solo speeches), singing, dancing, and magic were popular.

There might be up to 25 'turns' on one evening's bill.

In England, Music Halls presented lots of solo or small group acts. In France, Revues contained similar material but usually all performed by the same troupe of people.

American Vaudeville shows arose from entertainments like these.

Pantomime

The 19th century was the heyday of English pantomime, which derives from Commedia dell'Arte. In the 18th century, plays with music and dancing, featuring the story of the star-crossed lovers, Harlequin and Columbine, were brought to the English stage and called Harlequinades.

They began with a fairy story, then a magical character transformed the actors into their roles for the Harlequinade, which was the main attraction. The Harlequinade was usually satirical, meaning that it mocked public figures and political issues, and it featured clowning and slapstick, as in Commedia dell'Arte.

Later, the fairy tale became more important than the Harlequinade, and the satire was lost, although the comedy and clowning remained. Panto became a family entertainment associated with Christmas.

Traditions, such as men playing older, comic women, called dames, developed.

Women soon claimed the attractive "breeches parts" of the male heroes of the pantos.

Favourite pantomime fairy stories are The Babes in the Wood, Cinderella, Aladdin, Dick Whittington and so on.

Early 20th century

At the start of the 20th Century, there was a move towards realism. This was greatly influenced by people such as the Russian director Stanislavsky (pages 40-41) and author Chekhov (page 58).

Actors tried to act more naturalistically. They concentrated on psychological truthfulness in their portrayals. Sets were made to look as realistic as possible.

The play as a whole was considered more important than individual actors.

This more naturalistic style was the beginning of what most people recognize as good acting today.

With realism came the "fourth-wall" technique, in which the set forms three walls of a room. It is as if the fourth wall is removed to let the audience see in.

Theatre today

The second half of this century has been a time of experimentation, including reviving styles from other periods. Here are some of the features that characterize theatre today:

● The director is now usually a separate figure from the actors and his interpretation of a play is very important.

● To compete with television and cinema, theatre tries to exploit what is special about live performances, such as interaction with the audience.

● Since Brecht (pages 42-43), some people feel that theatre has a strong social or political role in society.

● Computers can now create extraordinary effects in staging and lighting. Classic plays, such as Shakespeare's, are constantly seen in new, sophisticated productions.

The fringe

Since the 1960s, plays not thought suitable for established theatres have been put on cheaply in rooms and halls and been called fringe theatre, as they are not mainstream. Many fringe plays tackle controversial issues. Some are so successful that they are later put on in commercial theatres.

Oriental theatre

This century, many Western writers and directors have been influenced by aspects of theatre from other cultures, especially Oriental. There is a long, and very different, tradition of theatre in China, Japan and other Eastern countries.

Japanese Noh theatre

Noh dates from the 14th century and has its roots in Buddhist and Shinto religious rituals, combined with popular entertainments. Noh is always performed on a stage like the one shown on the right.

The only scenery is a painted pine tree.

The main area is square with a roof like a temple.

The ato za is for musicians.

The hashigakari is a roofed way going backstage to the kagami no ma (mirror room) where actors study their masks before going on.

A chorus supports the leading actors. Where they sit is called the juitai-za.

Tradition

There are five schools of Noh (see left), each with its own repertoire and style. In 1647, a law was passed that each school must maintain its own traditions. Since then, tradition has been a constant theme of Noh.

KANZE
KOMPARU
KONGO
HOSHO
KITA

These are the names of the schools of Noh.

Actors wear sumptuous costumes and masks and use ritualized stances and gestures.

Noh masks are works of art made by specialist wood carvers.

The actors

By tradition, actors are male and born of acting families. There are five main character types: old man, man, woman, warrior and demon. Actors specialize in one of them from a very early age.

Plays always have a principal (shite), a subordinate role (waki) and the companion (tsure). The shite may be a demon, warrior, wife or other character in different plays.

Actors move and talk slowly and ceremonially, using gestures and intonations learned from their teacher.

Most Noh characters wear masks, and use a grand, formal acting style.

Noh performances

There are about 240 Noh plays. Most date from the 14th and 15th centuries, though modern ones do exist.

Performances last five to six hours. They include several plays, with comic interludes, called kyogen, to provide light relief.

Actors wear medieval Japanese costume. The audience know all the stories and characters. They do not expect originality, but to witness an age-old ritual being enacted and passed on.

Kabuki

Kabuki derived from Noh and was founded in Japan at the start of the 17th century by an actress called Okuri, her warrior partner and a troupe of mainly young women. By mid-17th century it was very popular. Then it was decreed that only men could act in Kabuki, so it never developed into a naturalistic style.

Kabuki roles

As in Noh, Kabuki actors are male, usually born into an acting family and are taught by their fathers to perfect one type of role.

Actors start in children's roles, then, for example, an actor called an onnagata, like the one on the right, will specialize in women's roles.

In a wig, painted face and gorgeous costume, this onnagata can seem to be a beautiful, graceful woman.

He does not pretend he is a woman, but presents a feminine ideal in his movements and gestures.

Kabuki style

Kabuki features splendid sets and costumes. Actors do not wear masks, but use elaborate, dramatic make-up. The colours and styles of make-up and wigs indicate a character's rank and degree of good or evil.

Manly make-up

Crab make-up

Here are some traditional painted Kabuki faces.

The Kabuki stage is a platform, with a special feature called the hanimichi, which is a narrow walkway running from the stage to the back of the theatre, through the audience.

Kabuki roles

tachiyaku: hero

katakiyaku: villain

kashagata: old woman

wakaonnagata: young woman

wakashugata: young man

oyayikata: old man

dokegata: comedian

Hanimichi

The hanimichi allows close contact with the audience and is a very dynamic use of space.

Leading actors often enter by the hanimichi and strike a mie (pose) here, for applause.

Wicked court noble

Kabuki tends to be more lighthearted than Noh, but it is still stylized and actors say their lines directly to the audience.

A special feature of Kabuki are the koken, stage assistants who help the actors with their costumes and props on stage. The audience ignores them.

The koken dress unobtrusively in black and do not interrupt performances.

Balinese dance

Bali is a small Indonesian island where performance has always formed part of religious and everyday life. Balinese dances often re-tell Hindu myths and although they are not naturalistic in style, they are quite easy to understand.

Traditionally, there were strict rules about who could dance religious dances. For example, leather workers and animal slaughterers were forbidden to dance, dancers were not supposed to have scars and only certain dances could be performed by older or married women.

Every hand movement and turn of the head means something in the dance "language".

Today, many of these conventions have lapsed. Dancing is a major tourist attraction, most of the dancers are professionals and the old rules no longer apply.

Peking Opera

This Chinese theatre form began in the 19th Century as a mixture of classical and popular forms of entertainment. It features acrobatics, operatic singing, dancing and dialogue.

Unlike in other Oriental forms, women take part in Peking Opera.

The stories have many sources, such as myth, history and fiction. They are usually melodramatic and have clear-cut, happy endings.

Music has a key role in Peking Opera. Each performance starts with a cymbal clash and banging gong. The orchestra on stage punctuates speech and movement as well as accompanying songs.

Large gong

Cymbals

The white face of this actor indicates that he is a clown.

Opera traditions

As in the other Oriental forms described here, colourful costumes and exotic make-up are used to denote characters' rank and personality.

Lots of percussion instruments (ones that are hit or banged together) are used in Peking Opera.

The Chinese lion, played by two actors, features in many stories.

A modern theatre

When a new theatre is built today, a lot of thought and planning go into it. A theatre is very expensive to build and run, so to attract a lot of customers it must be a convenient, welcoming place, offering a wide choice of entertainment.

The building

A brand new theatre building usually has two or more auditoria to allow several plays to be performed in the same time period (see how this works on the next page).

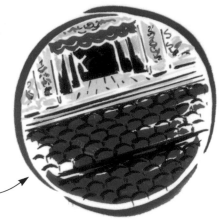

One auditorium usually has a proscenium arch stage. There is always a call for Classic plays to be performed in a traditional way in a space like this.

A bigger, open stage space allows the director more flexibility in all aspects of a production.

In a small studio, intimate and experimental productions that may not attract so many people can be tried without too much expense.

Backstage there are rehearsal rooms, wardrobes, workshops, dressing rooms and offices.

Public places are comfortable and well-designed. You can eat and drink in restaurants and bars, and buy books and souvenirs in shops. Leaflets and posters for future events are on display.

The theatre must be well served by public transport and have lots of parking space. Access for the disabled must also be planned.

The people

A large theatre complex is a big business employing lots of people. These are some of them.

- A director general or general manager is in overall charge.

- Artistic directors oversee the creative side.

- Each auditorium may employ up to twenty actors, with a resident director. Guest actors and directors may be invited for individual shows.

- Each auditorium also has its own stage crew: stage manager, lighting and sound technicians, costume and props people and so on.

- The financial director must ensure that the theatre is run at a profit.

- Accountants and financial staff keep track of costs and budgets.

- Marketing and design people produce programmes, leaflets, posters and the like.

- Front of house staff sell programmes, show people to their seats and serve in bars and shops.

- Box office staff sell tickets. Today, they often use a complex computer system and book several shows at a time over a period of months.

Planning the programme

The theatre's directors plan a year's programme in advance. They try to make the best use of the auditoria and to choose plays that will attract large audiences, but also to allow room for new works whose success is less certain.

Playing in rep

For variety and choice, programmes often play in repertory, or rep. This means that several plays swap around, playing for a few nights, taking a break, then coming back again. This calls for regular setting and striking of scenery and excellent organization to move and store sets safely and tidily.

Foyer entertainment

Music or other live entertainment in the foyer, short early evening performances and art exhibitions in a gallery space all add to a rounded programme of events.

Touring

The theatre may plan two or three shows which could be taken on tour in the region. These plays must be suitable for performance in other venues in towns that do not have a theatre.

Money matters

In most countries, large regional theatres receive government grants. Some find money in other ways, too:

Sponsors give the theatre a large sum of money each year in return for free tickets and other perks.

Corporate members (usually companies) book a number of seats at every performance during the year.

Individual membership does not cost much and allows you to book before anyone else.

Looking to the future

Most modern theatres are eager to encourage young playwrights. This is to ensure that there will always be good new plays to perform. Theatres that are well-known for presenting works by untried authors are sent hundreds of scripts to read every week by hopeful writers.

Readers sift them and pick out the best ones. These are then judged by a committee and one or two of them may be performed. Plays may also be commissioned from well-known authors.

Theatre in education

It is very important to encourage young people to enjoy theatre as they are the audience of the future. Large theatres have an education department where projects are planned to take to schools. These might include extracts from a play on the exam syllabus, or sketches on a history topic, for example.

Theatre in Education (T.I.E.) groups usually try to involve the children in their productions and hold workshops and discussions afterwards. They often leave a pack of materials relating to the play with a teacher, who can then follow up work on the subject in later drama lessons.

20th century influences

In the 20th century there has been no single, dominant theatre style. Instead, there have been lots of different ideas of what theatre could and should be like. Here are some of them.

Naturalism

At the end of the 19th century, scientists and philosophers became interested in the idea that where and how people lived and worked influenced how they thought and behaved.

Naturalism in novels and plays reflected this interest by showing characters' backgrounds in great detail.

Thérèse Raquin, a novel by Frenchman, Emile Zola, was the first influential naturalist work.

Stanislavsky was much influenced by naturalism.

Strindberg, Ibsen, D.H. Lawrence and G.B. Shaw all emphasised the circumstances of characters' lives.

Agit-prop

This is short for agitational propaganda, a political kind of theatre that appeared during the Russian Revolution and grew between 1917-1921. Actors acted out and explained recent political events to convince people that the revolution was right, and accept it.

During the 1920s-30s, agit-prop groups emerged all over Europe and the USA. In the 1960s-70s, there was a revival, especially in Britain.

The Moscow Blue Blouses were a famous agit-prop group. They called themselves a "living newspaper" for audiences who could not read.

Their performances were a mixture of sketches, songs, dance and acrobatics.

The kinetic stage

Kinetic means moving. A kinetic stage set was the idea of Edward Gordon Craig, an Englishman who started work in the theatre in 1889.

Craig rejected naturalism. He wanted sets to provide a background that moved and changed with the shifting moods of a play. Striking lighting, sound and acting style were all simply elements in the stage image.

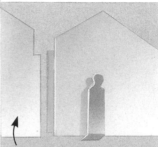

Moving screens in Craig's design for Hamlet at the Moscow Arts Theatre in 1912.

Craig's ideals were expensive and hard to make work. His writings and sketches are more influential than anything he actually did.

Theatre of Cruelty

French author Antonin Artaud was linked with the Surrealists, a group of artists who were fascinated by the power of people's subconscious thoughts and dreams.

He had ideas for a theatre that would stir these thoughts. In 1926 he founded his own theatre to try them out. It was not a success, so he returned to writing.

In his book *Theatre and its double* (1938) he first talked of a Theatre of Cruelty. It was to overwhelm people with action, light and sound and shock them into awareness of their subconscious desires.

Artaud never really succeeded in putting his ideas fully on stage, but his writing inspired many directors, including:

Charles Marowitz (USA), Jerzy Grotowski (Poland), Arianne Mnouchkine (France), Luca Ronconi (Italy), Peter Brook (UK).

Marat/Sade

In his 1964 production of Weiss's play *Marat/Sade*, Peter Brook tried to achieve a performance close to Artaud's ideals.

Theatre of the Absurd

After World War II, many writers felt that life had lost its meaning. Some wrote plays in which characters could not make sense of the world, or communicate, and outlandish things happened. These were often funny, as if that was the only way to cope with the tragedy.

Writers called Absurdist expressed the bleak sense of loss described by French philosopher Jean-Paul Sartre when he wrote about the feeling that life is absurd.

In Eugene Ionesco's *Rhinoceros*, the whole population of a town gradually turns into rhinoceroses.

In *Waiting for Godot*, Samuel Beckett's two tramps chat in a meaningless but funny way, waiting for non-existent Godot to tell them what to do.

Poor theatre

A Pole called Jerzy Grotowski coined the term poor theatre. He said that rich theatre tried to compete with television and film, and failed. 'Poor theatre' was to be stripped to its essentials.

Grotowski founded the Polish Theatre Laboratory in 1959, to search for new ways for actors to train and perform. He wanted to break down any inhibiting physical and mental barriers they had.

He rejected make-up, realistic scenery, props and costumes and focussed solely on the actor's body and craft.

After 1968 he did no more public performances, but still worked with actors.

Grotowski used methods from many sources: Stanislavsky, Brecht and Noh, for example.

In poor theatre every part of an actor's body had to be mobile and expressive.

The Theatre of Images

The Theatre of Images is the name given to the productions of American artist, Robert Wilson. He blends images, actions, sounds, dance and movements into stage "pictures" which people can interpret in any way they like.

Wilson worked with handicapped children and was fascinated by how children with brain damage manage to make sense of their world. His theatrical work is based on ways he found to help these children express themselves.

His productions are very long and slow. He intends people to get into a dream-like state and let the images flow over them.

His play, KA MOUNTAIN AND GUARDenia TERRACE was performed on Haft Tan Mountain in Iran in 1972. It ran for 168 hours.

Environmental theatre

Richard Schechner became professor of drama at New York university in 1967. Inspired by Jerzy Grotowski, he set up The Performance Group to improvise and perform plays.

His idea for an environmental theatre was that actors and audiences should share the theatre space and all take part in the performance.

Schechner wanted audiences to participate in and even to change the course of a play by things they said and did.

He left The Performance Group in 1972, but its work continued. In the mid-70s it changed its name to the Wooster Group (after the street the workshop is in) and it is now one of the best experimental groups in the USA under director Elizabeth LeCompte.

Going further

If you have enjoyed reading about acting and all the other aspects of theatre in this book, you may want to get involved yourself. If you are already in a drama group, you might be thinking of training for a job in the theatre. Here are some suggestions for ways to further an interest in drama.

Getting involved

The best way to start is in school. At some schools drama is on the timetable. At many more, there are theatre clubs after school. If there is no drama in your school, try asking a teacher you think might be interested, or even start a group yourself with some friends.

There are often theatre groups in local communities, in which people of all ages take part. The library, further education centres or a local newspaper are good places to find out more.

You do not have to work in the theatre professionally to continue a practical interest in it even after school or college. Amateur groups thrive and rehearse and perform at times that most working people can manage.

Youth theatres

In many countries there are youth theatre groups, often linked to a theatre. Young people of all ages take part. In some countries, a National Youth Theatre takes young people from all over the country and puts on performances of a high standard during the school holidays. Many successful actors get their first experience through these (see more on page 61).

Training for the theatre

Although theatre work may seem glamorous, it can be disheartening as a career. Competition for jobs is intense and many people spend long periods out of work. You need resilience, determination and luck, as well as talent, to succeed. Good training is the best way to make a start.

Where to train

Drama schools give you a professional training in a theatre skill, such as acting, set design, and so on. College or university drama courses give you an academic qualification and a broad insight into theatre along with some practical experience.

Applying to drama school

You can apply to drama schools straight after school, although many now prefer students who have done something else first, as they are more mature and less dazzled by the image of theatre.

Different schools run very different-style courses. Look carefully at prospectuses to make sure that they offer what you are looking for. Most courses last three years. There are some one-year courses for students who already have a college degree.

There may be two or more rounds of auditions for actors, which must usually be paid for, so be sure you are really keen before you apply. Technical applicants should be able to show some previous interest and involvement in their chosen field.

College and university

There is fierce competition for places so good academic results are often required.

Courses are usually for 3 or 4 years with a degree at the end. Written and theoretical work is done as well as practical, and courses are not a specialized training for a particular job in the theatre, as at drama school.

Theatre jobs

There are many ways of working in a theatrical environment. The best way to get jobs is often through contacts made at college or work experience in theatres.

Acting

National and local theatre companies usually employ actors on contract for one or more 'seasons'. A season is a period with a programme planned in advance. It is often repertory work (see page 53), which provides lots of varied experience.

Groups of actors often set up their own small companies to tour fringe theatres, leisure centres and the like. The lucky ones may get grants from arts organizations or sponsorship from businesses.

Variety, cabaret and revue present lots of short acts on one bill. Performers often do comic or musical sketches. Shows may be booked for a summer season at a hotel, or in city clubs, for example.

Film and television work are much better paid than the theatre. Advertising pays good money, too.

There are opportunities in making videos for businesses, either to help train their staff or sell their goods.

Radio stations need actors for plays, serials and ads. Only the actor's voice is heard, but the material is often good and the work pays quite well.

Theatre in education (TIE) combines teaching and acting. Groups devise their own short plays on interesting topics, or do versions of plays on the school curriculum. They perform in schools.

Street theatre is performed outside, usually where crowds gather, such as tourist spots. A hat may be passed around for coins during or after the performance. Groups must find out if they need permission to perform.

Technical jobs

All technical jobs are highly skilled, so it is best to train on a specialist course. Most technicians get jobs by writing to theatre companies or through contacts. Set and costume designers can fairly easily move from theatre to film or television, but lighting and sound technicians need to re-train as equipment varies.

Directing

Some drama schools run directors' courses, but many directors have no formal training. They build up experience with college or fringe shows. One way to start is to be assistant to a director, who might take you on after an interview or seeing your work.

Many directors set up their own companies, or work freelance, doing one show for a company, then moving on.

There are a few more stable jobs, such as artistic director of a company, but these are hard to come by and involve administration, too.

Theatre administration

This means running a theatre company, including finances. It is a pressurized job, as theatre companies are notorious for having money problems. It helps to have a business qualification as well as a theatrical background. Some colleges offer Arts administration courses.

Teaching

Drama is taught in schools, colleges and universities. To teach it, you usually need a teaching qualification or a drama degree. It also requires an all-round interest in theatre.

Actors' agent

An agent helps actors to get auditions and jobs. Agents scout around drama schools for promising actors to represent, then put them forward for suitable jobs. In return they get a percentage of the actors' earnings. Many agents are ex-actors, since extensive contacts in the theatre are essential.

Drama therapy

Drama therapy uses drama methods to help people to explore and overcome their psychological problems.

Drama techniques are also used in speech therapy.

You need to train on specialist courses to work as a therapist.

Who's who of playwrights

This list gives basic information about the world's best-known playwrights and names some of their most famous plays.

Aeschylus. 525/4-456BC. Ancient Greece. Tragedy. *The Oresteia* (458BC), a trilogy including *Agamemnon, The Choephori* or *Libation Bearers* and *The Eumenides.*

Albee Edward. Born 1928. USA. Sometimes associated with the European Absurdists. *The Zoo Story* (1959), *Who's Afraid of Virginia Woolf?* (1962).

Anouilh Jean. Born 1910. France. Tragi-comedy. *Antigone* (1944), *The Rehearsal* (1950).

Aristophanes. 448-380BC. Ancient Greece. Comedy. *Lysistrata* (411BC), *The Frogs* (405BC).

Ayckbourn Alan. Born 1939. England. Comedy. *The Norman Conquests* (1974), *Bedroom Farce* (1977).

Beaumarchais Pierre-Auguste Caron de. 1732-99. France. *The Barber of Seville* (1755).

Beaumont Francis. 1584-1616; and **Fletcher** John, 1579-1625. England. *Philaster, or Love Lies Bleeding* (1609), *The Scornful Lady* (1613).

Beckett Samuel. 1906-89. Born in Ireland but lived mostly in France and wrote mainly in French. *Waiting for Godot* (1956), *Endgame* (1958).

Behan Brendan. 1923-64. Ireland. *The Quare Fellow* (1955), *The Hostage* (1957).

Behn Aphra. 1640-89. England. Restoration comedy. First English woman to earn a living by writing. *The Rover* (1678), *Oroonoko* (1695).

Bond Edward. Born 1935. England. Political theatre/Agit-Prop. *Saved* (1965), *Lear* (1971).

Boucicault Dion. 1820-90. Ireland. Most successful and prolific writer of melodrama in the 19th century. *London Assurance* (1841), *The Corsican Brothers* (1855).

Brecht Bertolt. 1898-1956. Germany. Political theatre/Agit-Prop. *The Threepenny Opera* (1928), *Mother Courage and her Children* (1941).

Brenton Howard. Born 1942. England. Political theatre. *Epsom Downs* (1977), *The Romans in Britain* (1980).

Büchner Georg. 1813-37. Germany. Precursor of modern theatre. *Danton's Death* (1835), *Woyzeck* (published 1879).

Calderón de la Barca Pedro. 1600-1681. Spain. *La Vida Es Sueno* (*Life's a Dream*, about 1638).

Camus Albert. 1913-60. France. Associated with Absurdists. *Caligula* (1945), *Le Malentendu* (*The Misunderstanding,* 1945).

Chekhov Anton. 1860-1904. Russia. Tragi-comedy. *The Seagull* (1896), *The Cherry Orchard* (1904).

Churchill Caryl. Born 1938. England. *Cloud Nine* (1979), *Serious Money* (1987).

Cocteau Jean-Maurice. 1889-1963. France. *Antigone* (1922), *Orphée* (1924).

Congreve William. 1670-1729. England. Restoration comedy. *Love for Love* (1695), *The Way of the World* (1700).

Corneille Pierre. 1606-84. France. Tragedy. *Le Cid* (1636), *Nicomède* (1651).

Coward Noël. 1899-1973. England. Principally comedy of manners. *Private Lives* (1930), *Blithe Spirit* (1941).

Delaney Shelagh. Born 1939. England. *A Taste of Honey* (1958).

Dryden John. 1611-1700. England. Restoration comedy. *The Rival Ladies* (1664), *Marriage à la Mode* (1671).

Eliot Thomas Stearns (T.S.). 1888-1965. Born in America. Lived in England. Tried to develop a form of tragedy based on Greek drama. *Murder in the Cathedral* (1935), *The Family Reunion* (1939, based on *The Oresteia* – see **Aeschylus**).

Euripides. 484-406BC. Greece. Tragedy. *Trojan Women* (415BC), *The Bacchae* (performed posthumously).

F

Feydeau Georges-Léon-Jules-Marie. 1862-1921. France. Farce. *L'Hotel du Libre Echange* (*Hotel Paradiso*, 1899), *A Flea in Her Ear* (1907).

Fo Dario. Born 1926. Italy. Political theatre/Agit-prop. *Accidental Death of an Anarchist* (1979), *Can't Pay? Won't Pay!* (1981).

Frayn Michael. Born 1933. England. Comedy. *Alphabetical Order* (1975), *Make and Break* (1980).

Frisch Max. Born 1911. Switzerland. Influenced by Brecht. *The Fire Raisers* (1958), *Andorra* (1961).

Fugard Athol. Born 1932. South Africa. Political/social writer. *The Island* (1973), *A Lesson from Aloes* (1980).

G

Genet Jean. 1910-1988. France. Associated with the Absurdists. *The Maids* (1947), *The Blacks* (1959).

Gems Pam. Born 1925. England. *Queen Christina* (1977), *Piaf* (1978).

Giraudoux Jean. 1882-1944. France. *Siegfried* (1928), *Intermezzo* (1933).

Glaspell Susan. 1876-1948. USA. Experimental. *Trifles* (1916), *The Verge* (1921).

Goethe Johann Wolfgang 1749-1832. Germany. The most celebrated and studied classical German playwright. *Iphigenie and Tauris* (1779), *Faust* (1790).

Gogol Nikolai. 1809-1852. Russia. Comedy. *The Government Inspector* (1842), *Marriage* (1842).

Goldoni Carlo. 1709-1793. Attempted to revive Commedia dell'Arte through his plays. *The Servant of Two Masters* (1743), *The Liar* (1750).

Gorky Maxim. 1869-1936. USSR. Naturalism. *The Lower Depths* (1902), *The Mother* (1910).

H

Handke Peter. Born 1942. Germany. Experimentalist. *Kaspar* (1968), *The Ride Across Lake Constance* (1972).

Hansberry Lorraine. 1930-1965. USA. *Raisin in the Sun* (1959).

Hare David. Born 1947. England. Political. *Knuckle* (1974), *Plenty* (1978).

Hauptmann Gerhart. 1862-1946. Germany. Naturalism. *The Weavers* (1892), *Rose Bernd* (1903).

I

Ibsen Henrik. 1828-1906. Norway. Naturalism/Symbolism. *Peer Gynt* (1867), *A Doll's House* (1879).

Ionesco Eugène. Born 1912. France. Absurdism. *The Chairs* (1952), *Rhinoceros* (1960).

J

Jarry Alfred. 1873-1907. France. Grotesque comedy, precursor to Absurdism and Surrealism. *Ubu Roi* (1896), *Ubu Cocu* (1898)

Jellicoe Ann. Born 1927. England. Community/historical. *The Spirit of My Mad Mother* (1958), *The Knack* (1961).

Jonson Ben. 1572-1637. England. Tragedy, comedy. *Volpone, or The Fox* (1606), *The Alchemist* (1610).

K

Kyd Thomas. 1558-1594. England. Revenge tragedy. *The Spanish Tragedy* (about 1585-9).

L

Lawrence David Herbert (D.H.). 1885-1930. England. Linked with Naturalism. *The Daughter-in-Law* (1912), *The Widowing of Mrs. Holroyd* (1914).

Levy Deborah. Born 1955. England. *Pax* (1985), *Heresies* (1986).

Lorca Federico García. 1898-1936. Spain. Best-known for the trilogy: *Blood Wedding* (1933), *Yerma* (1934), *The House of Bernarda Alba* (1945).

M

Maeterlinck Maurice. 1862-1949. Belgium. Symbolism. *Pelléas and Mélisande* (1892), *The Blue Bird* (1909).

Mamet David. Born 1947. USA. *American Buffalo* (1975), *A Life in the Theatre* (1977).

Marivaux Pierre Carlet de Chamblain de. 1688-1763. France. Comedy. *La Double Inconstance* (1723), *L'Epreuve* (1740).

Marlowe Christopher. 1564-1593. England. Tragedy. *The Jew of Malta* (1589-90), *Dr. Faustus* (1590).

Mayakovsky Vladimir. 1894-1930. USSR. Revolutionary/political. *Mystery Bouffe* (1918).

Middleton Thomas. 1570-1627. England. Tragedy, comedy. *Women Beware Women* (1621), *The Changeling* (written with William Rowley, 1622).

Miller Arthur. Born 1915. American. Social drama/

modern tragedy. *Death of a Salesman* (1949), *The Crucible* (1953).

Molière Jean-Baptiste. 1622-1673. France. Comedy. *Tartuffe* (1667), *Le Bourgeois Gentilhomme* (1670), *The Hypochondriac* (1673).

O'Casey Sean. 1880-1964. Ireland. Political/social. *The Shadow of a Gunman* (1923), *Juno and the Paycock* (1924).

Odets Clifford. 1906-1963. American. Political/social. *Waiting for Lefty* (1935), *Golden Boy* (1937).

O'Neill Eugene. 1888-1953. USA. Modern tragedy. *Mourning Becomes Electra* (1931), *The Iceman Cometh* (1946).

Orton Joe. 1933-1967. England. Farce/satire. *Entertaining Mr. Sloane* (1964), *What the Butler Saw* (1969).

Osborne John. Born 1929. England. Social/political. *Look Back in Anger* (1956), *The Entertainer* (1957).

Page Louise. Born 1955. England. *Salonika* (1982), *Golden Girls* (1984).

Pinero Arthur Wing. 1855-1934. England. Comedy/farce. *The Magistrate* (1885), *Trelawny of the Wells* (1898).

Pinter Harold. Born 1930. England. "Comedies of menace". *The Caretaker* (1960), *The Homecoming* (1965).

Pirandello Luigi. 1867-1936. Italy. Comedy. *Six Characters in Search of an Author* (1921), *Tonight We Improvise* (1929).

Plautus. About 254-184BC. Ancient Rome. Comedy.

Menaechmi, Amphitruo (dates not known). **Shakespeare** and **Molière** drew on his works.

Priestley John Boynton (J.B.). 1894-1984. *An Inspector Calls* (1946).

Pushkin Alexander Sergeivich. 1799-1837. Russia. *Boris Godunov* (written 1819, published 1825, performed 1870).

Racine Jean. 1639-1699. France. Tragedy. *Andromaque* (1667), *Phèdre* (1677).

Rattigan Terence. 1911-1977. England. His plays were renowned as "well-made". *French Without Tears* (1936), *The Browning Version* (1946).

Robins Elizabeth. 1862-1952. USA. Political/Suffragette writer. *Alan's Wife* (1893), *Votes for Women* (1907).

Sartre Jean-Paul. 1905-1980. France. Philosopher associated with the Absurdists. *The Flies* (1942), *Huis Clos* (1944).

Schiller Friedrich. 1759-1805. Germany. *The Robbers* (1782), *Wilhelm Tell* (1804).

Seneca Lucius Annaeus. About 4BC-65AD. Roman. Tragedy. *Hippolytus, Thyestes* (nodates).

Shakespeare William. 1564-1616. England. Most studied, performed and influential British playwright. Tragedies include *Hamlet* (about 1600), *Othello* (1604), *King Lear* (1606), *Macbeth* (about 1606). Comedies include *A Midsummer Night's Dream, Much Ado About Nothing, Twelfth Night, As You Like It* (all 1595-1599).

Shaw George Bernard. 1856-1950. Ireland. Naturalism/social. *Mrs. Warren's Profession* (1893), *Pygmalion* (1914).

Shepard Sam. Born 1943. USA. Experimentalist. *The Tooth of Crime* (1973), *Buried Child* (1978).

Sheridan Richard Brinsley. 1751-1816. England. Comedy of manners. *The Rivals* (1775), *The School for Scandal* (1777).

Sophocles 496-406BC. Greece. Tragedy. *Oedipus the King* (about 429BC), *Antigone* (442-441BC).

Soyinka Wole. Born 1934. Nigeria. Political satire. *Madmen and Specialists* (1971), *Death and the King's Horseman* (1975).

Stoppard Tom. Born 1937. England. Comedy. *Rosencrantz and Guildenstern are Dead* (1967), *Travesties* (1975).

Strindberg August. 1849-1912. Sweden. Naturalism/Realism. *Miss Julie* (1888), *To Damascus I and II* (1898-1904).

Taylor Tom. 1817-1880. England. *The Ticket-of-Leave Man* (1863).

Toller Ernst. 1893-1939. Germany. *The Machine Wreckers* (1922), *Hoppla, wir leben!* (1927).

Travers Ben. 1886-1980. England. Farce. *A Cuckoo in the Nest* (1925), *Plunder* (1928).

Turgenev Ivan. 1818-1883. Russia. First psychological drama in Russian theatre, forerunner of Chekhov. *A Month in the Country* (1850).

Vanburgh Sir John. 1664-1726. England. Restoration comedy.

The Relapse; or Virtue in Danger (1696), *The Provoked Wife* (1697).

van Itallie Jean-Claude. Born 1936. USA. Experimentalist. *American Hurrah!* (1966), *The Serpent* (1968).

Vega Lope Félix de. 1562-1635. Spain. Huge influence in development of Spanish drama. *Fuenteovejuna (The Sheep-Well,* about 1612), *El Mejor Alcade El Rey (The King the Best Magistrate,* about 1620).

Webster John. About 1580-1634. England. Tragedy. *The White Devil* (1612), *The Duchess of*

Malfi (1614).

Wedekind Frank. 1864-1918. Associated with Symbolism. *Spring Awakening* (1891).

Wertenbaker Timberlake. Birthdate not given. Still alive. England and USA. *The Grace of Mary Traverse* (1985), *Our Country's Good* (1988).

Weiss Peter. 1916-1982. Germany. Documentary/political. *The Marat/Sade* (1964), *The Investigation* (1965).

Wilde Oscar. 1854-1900. Irish, lived in England. Comedy/social satire. *Lady Windermere's Fan* (1892), *The Importance of Being Earnest* (1895).

Wilder Thornton. 1897-1975. USA. *Our Town* (1938), *The Skin of Our Teeth* (1942).

Williams Tennessee. 1911-1983. USA. Modern tragedy. *A Streetcar Named Desire* (1947), *Cat on a Hot Tin Roof* (1955).

Wycherly Sir William. 1640-1716. England. Restoration comedy. *The Country Wife* (1675), *The Plain Dealer* (1676).

Yeats William Butler. 1865-1939. Ireland. Founded modern Irish dramatic movement. *The Hour Glass* (1914), *The Player Queen* (1922).

Youth theatres

Here are some addresses you can contact to find out about youth theatres.

Australia – contact the Education Officer at: Queensland Arts Council, G.P.O Box 376, Brisbane QLD 4001.
Victorian Arts Council, 4, Prospect Hill Road, Camberwell, VIC 3124.
Regional Cultural Council, 97 South Terrace, Adelaide, SA 5000.
Arts Council of Australia – Northern Territory Division, P.O. Box 1277, Darwin NT 0801.
Arts Council of Australia – Tasmania Division, P.O. Box 723, Devonport, TAS 7310.
New South Wales Arts Council, P.O. Box Q98, Queen Victoria Building, Post Office Sydney, NSW 2000.

Canada Carole Tarlington, Vancouver Youth Theatre, 1722 West Broadway, Vancouver, British Columbia, V6J 1T7

Eire National Association for Youth Drama, 23, Upper Gardiner Street, Dublin 1, Eire.

Hong Kong Hong Kong Youth Theatre Company, 504 Grosvenor House, 114 Macdonnell Road, Hong Kong.

New Zealand Brian McNeill, Northland Youth Theatre, Box 929, Whangarei.
Rosie Belton, P.O. Box 28073, Christchurch.

Singapore Roger Jenkins, Stars – Singapore's Community Theatre, 21, Scotts Road, Singapore 0922, Republic of Singapore.

U.K. National Association of Youth Theatres, Resource and Development Centre, The Bond, 180-182 Fazeley Street, Birmingham, B5 5SE.

Superstitions

Never wish an actor "Good luck"; it brings the opposite. You can joke by saying, "Break a leg", instead.

Never have real money, flowers, jewellery, food or mirrors on stage. It's impractical anyway, as they might spill or get lost or broken.

Never quote from Shakespeare's play, *Macbeth.* Many mishaps have occured to actors performing in *Macbeth* so it is thought very unlucky. People say "the Scottish play", instead.

Never whistle in the theatre. This could be because scene-shifting

signals used to be whistled, and any other whistles caused havoc.

The superstition, "good dress rehearsal, bad first night" probably arose because if the dress rehearsal goes too well, people don't concentrate enough at the first performance.

Some actors refuse to say the last line of a play at rehearsals. It makes the play "perfect", which tempts Fate to spoil it.

Some colours are bad luck. For instance, black is linked with death; yellow was the colour of the Devil in Medieval plays.

Glossary

This book explains the meanings of many theatre words. Here are some more terms you may hear. If you cannot find a word you don't understand here, look for it in the index, it is probably described in another part of the book.

apron Part of the stage that extends into the audience. A stage with a large apron is often called a thrust stage.

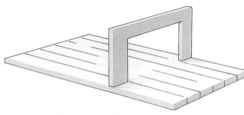

auditorium Seating area for the audience. In traditional theatres, often divided into sections, like this:

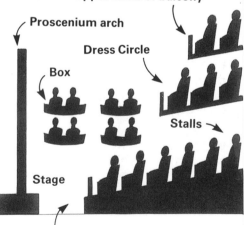

Upper circle or balcony

Proscenium arch

Dress Circle

Box

Stalls

Stage

Pit (for musicians to sit in),

balcony See **auditorium**.

bar or **barrel** Iron pipe above the stage from which lights and scenery are hung.

border a. Curtain used to hide lights. **b.** Curtain or plywood covering the front of rostra used to extend the stage.

box See **auditorium**.

circle See **auditorium**.

corpsing Uncontrollable laughing or fit of the giggles from an actor on stage.

curtain call When the audience claps at the end of the play and the actors return to take a bow.

cut-out Cloth cut out and shaped to make foliage or other irregular-shaped scenery. A cut-out flat is the same, only made of wood.

dock Storage area for scenery, usually backstage.

downstage See **stage directions**.

dress circle See **auditorium**.

front-of-house lighting Lights shining from above the auditorium onto the front of the stage.

FX Short for sound effects. Effects in a play may be labelled FX1, FX2 and so on by the DSM.

gauze Filmy cloth, used to create different effects depending on how it is lit. When lit from above and in front, gauze is opaque. Lit from behind, it becomes transparent. This change of lighting can be used to make something behind a gauze

suddenly appear, or cause something painted on the gauze to be revealed. Often used for magical or mysterious effects.

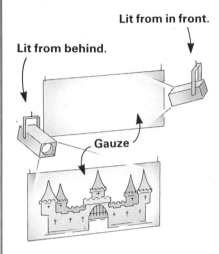

Lit from in front.

Lit from behind.

Gauze

gods The very highest galleries in a theatre.

green room Room backstage in which actors gather before and after performances. The first one is said to have been painted green.

grid Usually a steel framework above the stage from which equipment is hung.

ham Exaggerated overacting.

house lighting Lights above the auditorium, which are normally dimmed when a show commences.

limelight Greenish light shed by burning lime in lamps that were once used on stage. It was much brighter than other light sources at the time, so actors vied to be "in the limelight", that is, the centre of attraction.

lines Ropes of hemp or steel for raising and lowering scenery, usually by pulley.

LX Short for light effects. Effects may be numbered, LX1, LX2 by the DSM.

masking Cloth or flats hiding parts of the stage or backstage from the audience.

pit See **auditorium**.

priming An undercoat of a liquid called prime, or paint, used to prepare a flat before it is painted.

prompt Person who follows the play in the script and reminds an actor of his next words, if he forgets them. Not usually used in performances, nowadays, but the job may be done by the DSM at rehearsals.

rake The slope of the stage floor from **upstage** down towards the audience. Allows actors to be seen better.

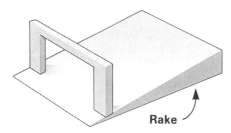

Rake

revolve Circular part of the stage floor that can be rotated by machinery below-stage. Often used for quick scene changes: two different scenes are set up on the two halves of the revolve. It rotates to change from one to the other.

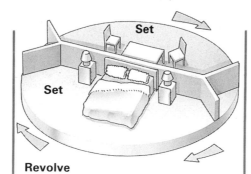

Revolve

safety curtain or **iron** Iron, or fireproof, sheet lowered between stage and auditorium to prevent the spread of fire.

stage cloth Cloth laid on the stage, or on the floor to create an acting area; painted for effect or used to deaden sound.

stage directions Instructions to describe fairly precise positions on stage. Authors may specify which position a character should move to, and the director uses the terms to tell actors where to go.

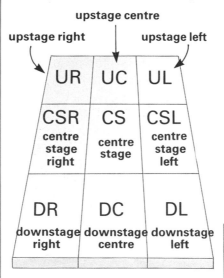

upstage centre
upstage right   upstage left

UR	UC	UL
CSR centre stage right	CS centre stage	CSL centre stage left
DR downstage right	DC downstage centre	DL downstage left

stage door Door, usually at the back or side, by which actors enter the theatre.

stage left, stage right See **stage directions**.

stalls See **auditorium**.

tabs Another word for curtains. The curtains across the front of the stage may be called front or house tabs.

Thespian Actors are sometimes called Thespians after an Ancient Greek called Thespis, said to have been the first person to step out from the Chorus to perform as a solo actor.

thrust stage. See **apron**.

trapdoor Small area of the stage floor that can be raised and lowered by machinery underneath. Used for actors to make entrances from or exits to below-stage.

Trapdoor

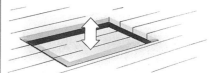

upstage a. See **stage directions. b.** To distract attention from someone further downstage.

wings Areas at the side of the stage, masked by curtains or flats, from which actors make their entrances.

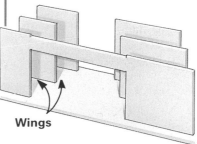

Wings

Index

First published in 1992. Usborne publishing Ltd, Usborne House, 83-85 Saffron Hill, London EC1N 8RT, England. Copyright © 1992 Usborne Publishing Ltd.